VILLAIN ERA

GODDESS

Release fears, set boundaries, build confidence, unleash your inner goddess.

Ashley Kim

DOWNRITE CHARMING

Printed in the United States of America.

For more information, or to book an event, contact:
http://www.villaineragoddess.com

Book design by Ashley Kim
Cover design by Ashley Kim

ISBN - Paperback: 979-8-218-51654-3
ISBN – E-book: 979-8-218-51655-0

First Edition: December 2024

DEDICATION

To the troublemakers—even if it's just quietly in your heart and not at the top of your lungs in the middle of the grocery store.

To Medusa, Eve, Lillith, Jezabel, Boudica, and *you*, dear reader, because I know the stories weaved around you weren't true either.

To my big sister, Jessica. I'm glad you're mine and I'm yours. You're perfect, don't make me tell you again.

Contents

INTRODUCTION

First, I need to admit that I'm totally a screamer. On rollercoasters. But we'll get to that in a bit.

You may be wondering what qualifies me to write this book. I'm not a doctor or reiki healer or a psychologist or counselor or a yogi, and I don't play any of those on the Internet either (although for the right price I totally would). I'm not qualified on paper to offer mental health advice. So why did I write this book? Who the hell am I? Who gave me the authority?

Well. Me. I did. I gave myself permission to write this book.

Because life is that first big drop on the scariest rollercoaster where you're plastered to your seat and your stomach is somehow lodged down in your feet and stuck up in your throat at the same time and you can't catch your breath. You can only hang on. And during this drop at 150 miles per hour, you're offered advice on how to ride roller coasters. From every direction. With all the contradictions and polarizing opinions. And it's all freaking overwhelming.

So while I'm not qualified to be your mental health counselor, I have ridden roller coasters.

Word of warning—if you're looking for a professional, smart-sounding, big-word-vomiting book of advice, then you're going to want to burn this piece of trash.

This book is the late-night conversations with girlfriends that happen in a half-rage-whisper while you're clutching your third glass of wine and you're sharing your stories while listening to theirs. In these freeing, honest moments, the pieces of hurt you've held onto start to fall off your back and you find some relief.

As you start sharing your truth, you may find there's an urgent need for something to change that bubbles up inside you. It gets closer to the surface each time you're allowed a safe space to voice your truth. And it's scary, because what happens when that need for change actually comes up to the surface? Will you change? Will your energy change? Will your voice change? Will the mask that you're wearing slip off? Will you be a big, freaking hot mess of a human?

Spoiler alert. The answer is yes to all of that. And that's why I wrote this book. Because it's messy and fucked up. But guess what? We can do it together.

Each time a friend has asked me "Well, how did you do it?" when I shared that I cut out toxic family members. Or they asked "Then what did you do?" when I tell them a family member left me hanging like bait on shark week. To answer those questions, I had to stop hiding and show them the brutal, embarrassing, hide-under-the-covers truth and inner work I used to wade through it. I had to do that for them. That change that bubbled up inside of me told me I have to do this. I have to write this book. This is the advice I needed, with the examples I needed, in the words I needed when I felt like I had no one. I'm sharing my messy journey with you, so you know you are not alone.

I'm sitting beside you on the rollercoaster, screaming my head off.

1. VILLAIN ORIGIN STORY

Let's get wild and scare the village folk.

I started this book, not to celebrate evil villains, but to liberate women from the villainous stories that are weaved around them as they fight each day to save themselves.

When we stop following the status quo set by family, by society, by our cultures . . . we become the villains.

Everyone has a different story about what stopped them in their tracks and made them start standing up for themselves and their families. With those actions come stories of our odd, rude, out-of-no-where behavior that spread through our families and communities like wildfire. "She wasn't raised to act like that!" We are terrifying and unpredictable to those around us. We stop laughing at jokes, become a little louder when speaking up, start saying "no" more often, stop answering phone calls, and start setting boundaries. Family, friends, co-workers, religions . . . they stop having free rein over us. They were so used to stretching out comfortably and hogging all of the space in our minds and bodies that when *we* set boundaries, *they* feel victimized. "She has *never* treated me that way before! So rude!"

Their reactions really can make you feel like a villain! The tough skin you have to grow to protect yourself and family from *ongoing* bullshit, while also healing yourself from generational trauma, while setting systems in place to protect your kids, while also healing your kids from any damage you've done to them before you started healing, is a lonely and difficult path. The relentless work we do to stay strong, to stick with our boundaries, to protect ourselves and our families, turns us into something that looks villainous from the outside.

I could always be counted on in my pre-villain era. I was very well trained. My family knew I'd be the one to make everyone feel comfortable. I'd be funny, kind, welcoming, and make everyone feel special. That was always my role in my family. I was the peacekeeper doormat, ready to make everyone feel good. You just gotta step on me a little bit—that'll make me squeak out words and actions of appeasement. Everyone commented on how proud my mom must be! I was so sweet! Oh my gosh, *just so sweet*! I was the one who made everyone feel like their stories were worth listening to, that their needs were important and should be met first. I was offered up to family and friends. And they took all they could get.

I was happy to be in full doormat mode. Sure, I didn't understand why I had ongoing pain in my body, an upset stomach all the time, and I didn't understand why my life was ruled by depression and anxiety. I was being told I was "good" so I was happy. *Right???*

Girl. Let me tell you. I was not happy. I was good at following rules. Rules that weren't created *for* me. They were created to *use* me. I thought that being patted on the head for following those rules was my happiness.

My story is not unique. In fact, it might sound similar to yours. We were the good girls. Always smiling. Always ready to serve however we could. Even with scars on our bodies. Even with broken hearts. Even after abuse. Even with shame filling our bodies. We were the ones who could still be counted on.

All the more reason why our villain era is so shocking to our families!

I created this book because I didn't want to be alone. I didn't want to be alone while I navigate this journey. It's not fun being the villain by yourself. It's not fun being the one who is told you're letting the family down. It's not fun doing shadow work, having your eyes opened and then being forced to see people in a new light that isn't very flattering. It's not fun to shine a spotlight on shame to see where the hell it's coming from. I didn't want to be alone and I'm assuming you probably don't want to either. So, let's do this together.

This book contains exercises I used (and still use!), affirmations, and reminders of who you really are. A true goddess.

We'll be navigating the villain era like the true goddess we are, demanding nothing but the best for ourselves. Thank you for joining me on this journey. Are you ready to celebrate your villain era? Let's go!

LAUNCHING YOUR VILLAIN ERA

2. UNLEASH YOUR INNER VILLAIN

The fearless pursuit of selfishness.

"I'm a lover, not a fighter," but I can fight.

For too long, we've been living in skin that doesn't feel like our own. We've been applying our long-lash mascara, using our teeth whitening toothpaste, and acting like socially acceptable humans for so long we've forgotten our inner goddesses need dirty feet, leg hair, and dresses with pockets to thrive.

Your villain era is here to save you. Like shadows seeking shelter under a weeping willow tree at midnight, this era was created to shelter your soul as you make the necessary adjustments around you. We're not killing people with kindness anymore. We're murdering long-held expectations while bathing in our true power. Are you ready? The body count will be high, but the reward is a life that is truly, honestly lived.

The Checklist for Being Socially Acceptable

What does your checklist for being socially acceptable look like? These are the rules you follow to limit judgment from others and to fit in so you don't ruffle feathers. We all have one carefully hidden away in our guts, calling the action shots.

After years of being molded by others and being taught *their* definitions of good and bad, my checklist was pretty extensive before I turned into a villain.

This is just a tiny part of a huge checklist I used to navigate life:

- Go to church every time the doors are open to prove I hold the same values as those around me, even if it means sacrificing the wellbeing of myself and my children.
- Get a promotion or raise once a year to prove my worth to those who are nosey enough to ask, even if it means sacrificing the wellbeing of myself and my children.
- Raise children who are so well-behaved that I get non-stop compliments, even if it means sacrificing the wellbeing of my children.
- Be a supportive wife and put myself last in all scenarios, even if it means sacrificing the wellbeing of myself.
- Attend all family events no matter who's there and the harm they've done to others, even if it means sacrificing the wellbeing of myself and my children.
- Be polite at all times, even if it means sacrificing the wellbeing of myself.
- Hold in emotions so others feel comfortable, even if it means sacrificing the wellbeing of myself.
- Be forgiving at all times, even if it means sacrificing the wellbeing of myself.
- Keep myself available to family at all times, even if it means

sacrificing my body, my mental health, and my boundaries.

In a society where conformity is rewarded, the need to fit in can quickly become your director, orchestrating your performance to maintain acceptance. Instead of reviewing my list objectively, I just kept adding to it every time I realized I didn't fit it. (Or—cringe—when I desperately wanted to fit in). It grew too big to even be manageable.

Conformity Feeds Off Fear

When being yourself is the worst thing you can be, it's scary to stand out. I was scared to be ostracized from my community for being the weird one who stood out for not following the rules. As I toyed around with even thinking about entering my villain era, I was scared I wouldn't blend into the background anymore. Not blending in meant less safety. I just wanted to stay in the shadows until it was time to perform, then go back into the dark corner.

Fear became my companion and the director of the show I called "Life." It guided me toward safety. I relied on it, like a long-time friend.

Fear is a Shitty Friend

Fear feels like a friend when it's all you know. But that bitch will always stab you in the back.

Sure, she'll offer comfort and be the first to pour you a shot of tequila after a rough day. But then she's going to pull out a long list of "what ifs" so you can't enjoy your drink.

Feeling fear is normal and familiar. Especially if you're raised with it. And giving up fear is scary. *Especially if you're raised with it.*

Not knowing the outcome before embarking on a journey is scary as hell. Even more so when you're entering your villain era and you know you're going to ruffle some feathers. There are zero guarantees that you'll have support from others while you navigate this new era.

At the end of the day, you have to ask yourself: Do I want false support, or do I want freedom? Because what if standing out and going against society's checklist of "good" was the key to freedom, protection, and happiness all along? What if ditching that two-faced friend, Fear, was the answer to taming the wild winds of this new era? What if we peeled away the "normal" skin and tried on the original skin we were born with?

Shapeshifting into "Selfish"

As I entered my villain era, redefining "good" was crucial to my survival. It meant becoming "selfish" and rewriting the checklist to protect myself and my family.

Realizing that I was the main character in my life, not just the supporting actress running around with a smile lifting up everyone else, gave me the permission I needed. The *selfishness* I needed. Permission to set my own rules that would protect me and my family. I've since updated the checklist:

Outdated expectations		Redefined with boundaries
Go to church every time the doors are open to prove I hold the same values as those around me, even if it means sacrificing the wellbeing of myself and my children.	»	I practice adding love and kindness to the collective in whichever way my intuition presents to me at the time.

Outdated expectations		Redefined with boundaries
Get a promotion or raise once a year to prove my worth to those who are nosey enough to ask, even if it means sacrificing the wellbeing of myself and my children.	»	I will earn enough to give my family opportunities.
Raise children who are so well-behaved that I get non-stop compliments, even if it means sacrificing the wellbeing of my children.	»	I allow my children to be messy and embarrassing as they learn life lessons that'll set them up to be successful adults.
Be a supportive wife and put myself last in all scenarios, even if it means sacrificing the wellbeing of myself.	»	I will be a partner in a relationship where someone has my back as much as I have theirs.
Attend all family events no matter who's there and the harm they've done to others, even if it means sacrificing the wellbeing of myself and my children.	»	I will show my kids how to put themselves first in a situation that makes them feel uncomfortable, even if it means upsetting family.
Be polite at all times, even if it means sacrificing the wellbeing of myself.	»	I will treat you respectfully within my boundaries.
Hold in emotions at all times, even if it means sacrificing the wellbeing of myself.	»	I will not bear the weight of other people's emotions and will react accordingly.

Outdated expectations		Redefined with boundaries
Be forgiving at all times, even if it means sacrificing the wellbeing of myself.	»	Everyone has a bad day once in a while. However, any action taken three times or more is a pattern, and you don't deserve forgiveness or forgetfulness on my part.
Keep myself available to family at all times, even if it means sacrificing my body, my mental health, and my boundaries.	»	I want to be helpful, but at the end of the day I will do what I can, when I can, for my extended family.

As you can see, my list changed from centering around everyone outside of my household to centering around my immediate family first. I also started placing my family's growth, messiness, and desires above "looking good in public."

Create Your Own Acceptable List

It's time to emerge from the dark corner where you were performing your wallflower act and rewrite the script. Redefining what "good" means to you will be your roadmap for moving forward. These are the values that help protect you and your family as you venture back into the world as a villain.

Word of warning, this is when the "villain" label gets slapped on your back by family, friends, coworkers, and everyone else who enjoyed your conformity. But it's worth it!

After redefining "good" and creating my own list of rules to live by, I realized one of my most controlling fears was that I would make someone feel uncomfortable. I had been responsible for the emotions of others for so long, I didn't realize I was bending myself backwards until I broke in half just to make sure I didn't make anyone else uncomfortable.

This activity is great for those of us who were woven into being little doormats. Realizing that I wasn't responsible for the comfort or emotions of others was a huge step in boundary setting for me and came with tons of relief.

When you first start this list, I recommend sitting down to focus all of your energy on this task. You'll keep adding to it over time as things come up, but to get started, focus only on this.

Here are some categories to think about when creating your own "Acceptable and Good" list:

The Kill You Slowly category
- o These are times you say "yes" even though it slowly kills you inside. This could be letting others take advantage of you. Or following someone's values that aren't your own.
- o When do you do things you absolutely dread?

The Cringe and Hide category
- o If you're guilted into the "blood before water" bullshit every time you want to avoid icky family members, then this category is for you!
- o When do you want to cringe and hide but instead act like everything is fine and move forward, following directions anyway?

The Fake as Shit category
- o This includes anytime you're not being your authentic self or are participating in something you don't fully believe in.
- o You may be participating because you might let someone down or be judged if you didn't.

Your New Acceptable and Good List

Outdated expectations	Redefined with boundaries
»	
»	
»	
»	

Keep working on your list, give yourself grace and patience, and don't judge yourself. Feel free to share with others what you're doing. Your family and friends will see a shift in you, and open communication can help prevent misunderstandings with those you love.

Redefining your "Acceptable and Good" list is a great way to get started by ensuring your decisions aren't based on fears.

Now, let's look at confronting your fears.

Fear Versus Intuition

You might not remember this, but when you were born, you had this glowing, gold spark in your belly called "intuition." It was slowly beat down into a tiny, flickering spark, until it was eventually snuffed out by family, teachers, religion, and society. This warm, soft, golden intuition was replaced by the dark, cold icicles of fear that rule your body.

We're brought up with fear being our first companion. This sneaky little bitch has been deeply ingrained within us and, unfortunately, continues to shape our decision-making processes as adults. These fears are ingrained in us through:

Home life and our parents

From "share your toys or else" to "cover up your body, there are men around," we're constantly hearing threats and warnings from parents. While I do agree there are things we should be warning our kids about, leading by threat and fear (instead of direction and love) launches a sandstorm of mistrust and fear that we're trying to walk through well into adulthood.

Many parenting styles are based on lording over kids with fear, not guiding kids with knowledge. The word "discipline" was warped to mean spankings and timeouts, not protection and lessons.

Traumatic experiences

As a society, we don't give people the space to recover from trauma. These high-handed, hold-you-down toads of the human world also control the narrative on how we deal with trauma and how we, as a society, look upon abusers after they've abused. These are the "forgive and forget," "don't hold a grudge," "mental illness just runs in the family," "what did you do to deserve it" assholes purposefully getting in the way of our healing.

We learn as young as toddlers that not only are our truths not safe, our truths are gobbled up by abusers who spit out a new story that we're forced to agree with. Physical and emotional abuse doesn't get a chance to leave our bodies. Instead, it gets packed down into our bones, leaking into our cells and feasting on our health.

Our perception of safety, trust, and self-worth is so distorted we think we're living a normal life. And we come in contact with *so many* others like us that we convince ourselves that maybe we *are* normal.

Society

The Stepford-Wives of society are always there to keep you in line. All our ideas of success and all the confusing and contradicting rules for how a woman conducts herself are steeped in the patriarchy and their religions, which, of course, was built on white supremacy. Women who are over the bullshit know what I'm talking about.

I'm still confused as to how somewhere in history, women got tricked into believing that they had to be literally everything to everyone all the time. Men get "man caves," women get a kitchen and house to clean. Men get careers, women get households to clean, children to raise, oh and jobs on top of all of that. Men get hobbies, women get to step in as caretakers for family and friends, run the kids to the doctor, meet with the school, and maybe after 10:00 p.m. if they're not tired, they can work on a hobby.

It's almost laughable at how absurd it is. There are women in our society who play important roles in holding other women down through religion and societal expectations. I'm not just blaming men. It's the entire system.

Let Intuition Speak First

Replacing fear with intuition is a slow process that doesn't happen overnight. You will need to get to know your body again. Pay attention to your body when you react out of fear. Pay attention to what your body felt like when you looked back and thought, *I* knew *that was going to happen.* Or *I knew something felt off about him.* Pay attention to what your body was doing at that moment.

It took months before I realized the difference between fear and intuition. Here's how it feels in my body:

Fear quickly spreads from the center of my chest to my shoulders like spiders with icicles for feet. It's a feeling that is all-consuming and difficult to ignore.

Intuition starts in my gut and feels more like a warm presence just sitting there. It's not flooding my body with sensation, but it will gently make itself known (it's also much easier to ignore).

These feelings aren't the exact same for everyone, but they are pretty similar. There's a reason people say "trust your gut," because that's where your intuition lives. And there's a reason why our shoulders hurt when we're stressed about something.

I think the better alternative when you're just starting to listen to yourself is to say "ignore your chest," because that feeling is the most intrusive and easier to recognize.

I recommend that you journal your experiences at the end of the day, documenting the changes in your body and what your decisions were. Over time, you'll see a pattern emerge.

Documenting your intuition and inner-guidance is a great way to get to know yourself, too. As a person who has dealt with anxiety and intrusive thoughts her whole life, I didn't believe I could elevate my inner guidance system over my survival of fear and anxiety, but once I started really celebrating my intuition and listening to my body, it got easier and easier.

Now, as soon as the icy little feet start crawling across my chest or up to my head, I recognize it as fear right away. I can sit back and assess the situation objectively and put more thought into what my decision should be.

Climbing Out of the Coffin

When you first give up being ruled by fear, you'll feel like you're missing a security blanket and you might react in ways you're not prepared for.

- Maybe you double down on your fear and second-guess yourself.
- Maybe you tell someone you're not making decisions out of fear anymore and they say you're being reckless.
- Maybe you get caught up in the moment, forget your anti-fear ways, and accidentally react by making a decision out of fear.

All of these scenarios are normal and you're still doing a great job. I've never met one person who set a goal or tried to change a habit and it worked the first day.

Just keep trying. You're not a failure. You're not a loser. You're not a bad mom, wife, co-worker, leader, bus driver, boss, sandwich artist, friend, parallel parker, whatever. This is a messy process, and your fine self is doing a great job. This is something you have to work on daily. I'm still working on it!

Keep reminding yourself that fear is not a security blanket. It's a coffin. And it's time to get out before the lid closes.

Taming Your Big, Bad Scaries

In my late twenties, I made my first ever New Year's resolution, and it was to stop making decisions out of fear.

When I had a decision to make about a new job or something equally important, I'd write my pros and cons list and then cross out anything that was related to a fear before making my decision. It was life changing—as in, I changed my life drastically. I stopped going to church. I got divorced. I moved to a different town. I quit my job (multiple times) when I wanted something better. I chose a partner based on living life to the fullest.

Moving toward a gentler life, guided by intuition and giving up the knee-jerk reactions led by fear, means you also have to tame your big, bad scaries.

Before you walk into a pet shop and ask to hold spiders for a bit of DIY exposure therapy, I'm not talking about phobias. The big, bad scaries are the fears that stop you from moving forward in life.

What scares you down to your bones? It usually isn't "fear" that scares someone. It's the outcome of a situation that they fear.

Here are some examples from myself and other women I've spoken to:

- Reliving memories of past childhood traumas.
- Negativity from others that might follow success.
- Being rejected by your parents after you set boundaries.
- Facing the wrath of your family tomorrow after standing up for yourself today.
- Losing close friends when you start being yourself.
- Being an outcast at work when you stop laughing at gross jokes and doing what it takes to fit in

Many women who've found out I'm writing this book are very uncomfortable with this part of the process. Facing their big, bad scaries is their worst nightmare.

It means admitting that this bandaid of keeping ourselves small isn't actually working. We're fucking miserable. And babe, I know that exposing your truest self and reclaiming what's yours feels far scarier than knowing you're losing yourself.

I can't tell you it's easy. It does feel worse… at first. But the key word is feel. It feels worse. But it isn't. It's better, and freedom is on the other side. So much freedom.

Be a Salty Bitch

There is one easy ritual you can perform to help you get into the badass mode and kick fear to the curb. And you're going to need salt.

If you're ready to start looking closer at your big, bad scaries and want to relinquish the control they have on you, this ritual is a safe way to start inner reflection with topics that might usually be too stressful.

This ritual involves writing your emotions, thoughts, and fears on a surface of salt and then symbolically erasing them. Physically writing them in salt forces you to focus on your thoughts. But writing in salt serves two other functions. One is to ensure what you've written is confidential because it can be erased. The other is that salt is a wonderful way to cleanse negative energy, making it a safe conduit for getting to know your shadow self. Here's how:

Secure a Safe Space

Find a quiet and comfortable space where you won't be disturbed. Set a plate or container in front of you and fill it with enough salt to write in. Remember that this process might bring up challenging emotions, so ensure you're in a safe and comfortable space before you begin.

Ground and Center Yourself

Take a few deep breaths, letting go of any distractions, and focus your attention on the present moment.

Let it All Out

If you have a specific choice or issue that you need to focus on, you can do that now. Otherwise, you can use some of these prompts to help you get started:

- What are you scared of right now?
- How will you judge yourself if you make a specific choice?
- How have you lost yourself to conformity this year?
- What's something you fear telling anyone?
- Is there something you want to say or do that you're holding back from doing?

Acceptance and Grace

Sit quietly and observe what you've written in salt. Accept it. Don't judge! Accept and love yourself with it.

Erase the Words

Take a deep breath, erase the words, and let the negativity you felt with those words be erased as well. Repeat as many times as you want or until you feel like you've had enough for the day.

Be Proud and Stay Strong

When you're all done, give yourself some gratitude for doing something that adults will literally spend their own whole lives running from. You shined a light on your big, bad scaries and can move forward with more control in your life.

Taking control of your scaries, means it's time to think about how you can work toward conquering them because you and I both know we can't just walk around scared all the time. It's time to create a plan.

Start by listing out your scaires. For example, if one of your big scaries might be "being rejected by your parents after you set boundaries."

Next, think about the ideal solution you want to work toward. So your solution could be "Setting your boundaries and having the conversations when needed" but that's scary as shit! Sure, you know that you must set boundaries, but that's scary, so you need to think through how you're going to protect yourself, too.

Your final step is to make a plan for how you're going to protect yourself. For the example above, you might write down something like "Have responses prepared, follow self-soothing practices as needed, journal to process emotions."

When you're just starting out you might not have come up with the ideas of "self-soothing practices" or "journal to process emotions" - that's ok! That's what this book is for! Your job right now is to download the worksheet "The Big Bad Scary List" and fill it out as you read this book. You won't have all the solutions and answers right away, but hopefully by the end, you'll have an amazing plan in place to move forward.

You did it! This chapter is one of the hardest because you're getting a glimpse at the work you need to do, but luckily villains are tough as hell (you can be tough and cry at the same time). I'm proud of you! Embrace the journey of releasing fear, conquering the big, bad, scary, and rewriting your story. The path to being your authentic self awaits, and you have the power to become the victor in this battle against fear.

👑 *I give you permission to pick up your sparkling sword and become the slayer of fears. I give you permission to launch into this ugly battle of defeating fear and reclaiming yourself. Your intuition, your heart, and your future is locked away in a castle and you're the savior. You're the victor. I know with all my heart and body that you'll walk off the battlefield with old, beat-up fears following you, tamed and quiet in your footsteps. You're now their master.*

I'M LED BY LOVE, NOT FEAR.

3. TRUSTING YOURSELF

Combat the tendencies to conform, confine, and constrain.

"I'm new here" and other thoughts you'll have after trusting yourself.

Trusting yourself is paramount to being able to glide through life with a bit more ease. Looking back at past mistakes, it's easy to feel underqualified for trustworthiness. You might look at your reflection in the mirror and think, "Why would I trust *this*?"

I write this book lying on the ground with dirty hands. Not while sitting on a cushy, clean pedestal. Not with birds singing and butterflies landing around me. And certainly not without messes and mistakes. I'm in the trenches. I'm muddy and I'm pulling my body through the filth that is life. I had babies in the mud. I grew my dreams in this mud. I will survive this mud. And I will do it in a way that makes me whole—which means trusting myself.

Turning Mistakes into Trust

When I started this journey, my self-worth was non-existent. I've had to learn that it's not being perfect that makes me trust myself. It's surviving the mud that made me trust myself. Yes, I made mistakes (lots of them). But after working to forgive myself, I can look past mistakes and focus on the lessons. Because guess what? The lesson after a mistake? It's usually *that if* I had listened to my inner voice, I wouldn't have made the mistake. Or it wouldn't have been as bad.

Everyone reading this book can remember a time when you didn't listen to your gut and went forward anyway. How many times have you said, "I should have listened to my gut" or "Something was telling me not to do that." Me, too! Way too fucking many! That feeling is your body screaming, "Bitch, I'm qualified! Trust me!" Those lessons gathered together equal a whole ton of experiences. It's not perfection that qualifies you to trust yourself. It's your experiences up to this point that *prove* you should trust yourself.

Let me tell you about my body, my gut, and my intuition protecting my babies. I had an uncle who creeped me out. I instinctively kept my kids away from him. Something in me screamed that I should pay attention to this gut feeling. When I say screamed, I mean *screamed*. I almost couldn't hear anyone talk over my own body yelling, "Grab your babies and get the fuck out." I didn't like being around him during my entire childhood, but I ignored the screaming inside, because I wanted to be a good girl and not rock the boat.

Tides turned. Once I had my own babies, I couldn't ignore it anymore. So I stopped visiting my parents if my uncle was there. And let me tell you, I paid the price. I was told I was rude. I tried to be honest with family members I felt close to and explain that I felt like he wasn't safe and I should keep my kids away. They were confused and offended. They didn't understand how I could stop hanging out with family because I had a *feeling* that I couldn't explain. I was being very offensive to family members based on made-up paranoia.

I was the villain.

For *years,* I was the villain. And sometimes I did question myself. Maybe I was being too rude? Maybe I was making this feeling up in my head? But I stayed with it. I had to—my body was *screaming* at me. Well, fast forward twelve years and guess what, honey. It came out that he had been molesting his nieces and nephews while we were growing up. The screaming inside my body? It was for a reason!

Did I handle this with grace? Ha! Not even close. I strutted around with "I told you so" swagger. I stood up straighter just so everyone could see the smug look on my face.

I'm not going to lie. Learning to trust yourself—your true self, not your fear—is *hard*. Your fear has been guiding you this whole time and now you have to trust your inner guidance? Trust your gut? You might be thinking, "What gut? What instincts?"

I can see why you're confused. Our instincts and everything we needed to trust ourselves were ripped away from us as babies.

- Especially if we grew up in religion.
- Especially if we grew up with abusers gaslighting us.
- Especially if you grew up with gaslit victims who follow the status quo and support the abusers.

Our instincts are buried so deeply we don't know what the voice of intuition inside our bodies sounds like. When our bodies react to something, we don't know if it's our intuition or if it's just fear of the unknown. For me, this was one of the hardest things to bring back to my life.

The Witch's Wound

Have you heard the term "witch's wound?" It's a term that refers to the generational trauma women carry after the mass execution of women in the Salem witch trials and other areas around the world.

The witch's wound is a psychological and spiritual wound that women still have to this day. It's passed down through our cells. Our bodies remember the betrayal that occurred all around the world to millions of women during this time. We were killed in horrific ways. You don't need to be a witch to identify with this trauma. You just need to be a woman.

The Salem witch trials were a warning to women that if you spoke too loudly, were a little different, or someone just didn't like you, then you were free game for the violent mobs. It is a reminder that lives deep in your bones that you need to be as small as you can and to be as agreeable as possible or anyone can turn on you—even other women. Remember, witches weren't burned at the stake—*everyday, normal women* were burned at the stake. Did your school clarify that? Mine sure didn't. Some call this mass execution of women "genderside"… Did your school teach you that one? Mine didn't either.

With a witch's wound constantly bleeding inside of us, it's almost impossible to trust ourselves. When distrust and fear of non-conformity greet you each morning as you try to walk your own unique path, you're going to feel like you're the one who's wrong.

Learning to trust yourself is one of the biggest steps you can take to save yourself from conforming, confining, and constricting yourself for others.

Be Quiet and Listen

The process toward trusting yourself starts with simply being quiet. Find a quiet spot, ignore your phone, and pay attention to *you*. Use this time to reflect, to journal, and to listen to yourself and all of your thoughts.

As you move forward, pay more attention to your body—where do you feel sensations? In your chest? In your tummy? Where is the first sensation? What's the sensation telling you?

Journal or meditate on those questions until you learn your body and your responses. Your goal is to connect with yourself and get to know *you* better.

Three-Day Answer Method

Use this trick to keep your decision making between you and your higher good (the universe, God, whatever you want to call it). You're going to think I'm just making shit up at this point, but I swear this works. If you're trying to make a decision and you're having a hard time knowing if you're trusting your intuition or if you're accidentally allowing outside influences to affect you. Try this:

1. Journal about what you need to decide or journal about how you're ready to make a change in your life and you're not sure what steps to take next.
2. Watch Pinterest or some other social app (one of the less stressful apps) for a few days (I give it three days), and I promise your answer will pop up within three days. I usually see an answer the next day.

Don't dwell on finding your answer, just keep living your life and chugging along. The universe will make sure the answer jumps right in front of your face when it happens. I like Pinterest because it's an app dedicated to idea generation anyway and doesn't seem to pull up stressful topics like other apps.

Just wait until you try it! No one believes me until they try it. If your answer doesn't come to you in three days, then the path wasn't for you. Done.

I give you permission to act like you're hot shit. You're the "trust my own damn self, decision-making queen" who doesn't need to follow anyone else's path. Sure, learning from others is great, but at the end of the day, you're celebrating yourself and your own journey.

4. FOLLOWING YOUR OWN PATH

Moving forward without outside validation.

External validation is an unreliable roadmap.

I remember the first time I realized I was an attention whore.

Have you gone through this realization yet? The realization that all of your internal guidance systems and cues were built around other people outside of you? We don't know if we're on the right track unless someone tells us. We don't know if we're a good person unless someone tells us. We don't know if we're valuable unless someone tells us. By looking outside of ourselves for this validation, we've turned into attention whores who need validation for every aspect of our lives.

My "awakening" happened when I was twenty-seven, sweating, seven months pregnant, and suffering from my sixth day of fighting pneumonia while proving what a hard worker I was by not taking a sick day.

I was fourteen months into a highly coveted job I had really, really,

really wanted. One of the head guys had taken me to lunch, and I had casually mentioned that I wished the company had a mentorship program. I told him that I felt like I could use some guidance.

He recoiled while setting down his messy, half-eaten Subway sandwich. Evidently, he needed both hands to let me know that anyone who relies on a mentor for growth will always be behind everyone else. That it was a crutch for not figuring it out for yourself. I didn't completely agree with him, but I did have a flashback to feedback from my previous manager during an annual review: "Ashley is a wonderful employee, but she seeks constant feedback." At the time of the review I thought, *Well, you're welcome. I'm glad I'm checking in with you to make sure I don't suck and bring the whole company crashing down.* But, no, she was politely trying to tell me that I was annoying as hell and I needed to stop asking her to act like my mommy. The funny thing is, I was thinking of her when I said I wished I had a mentor. Yikes.

Fast forward two years later when I'm sitting in a grimy Subway booth, wiping sauce off my hands, trying to inhale a six-inch sub in the most lady-like way possible while breathing through my mouth because my sick ass should have stayed home. I was shocked as hell to learn that my wanting guidance and feedback wasn't viewed as a positive trait. It actually made me look insecure.

It dawned on me that I needed constant validation with every little small step I took. I didn't want a mentor because I was ready to build my career. I wanted a mentor because I needed a work mom to give me constant validation.

Validation Comes from Within

I hadn't realized that validation can come from within. I didn't realize I could assess my own strengths and weaknesses and *trust* my self assessment.

I didn't think that I was allowed to think positive things about myself unless someone else said them first.

I wasn't pretty until someone else told me. I wasn't smart until someone else told me. I wasn't good at my hobbies until someone else told me. Otherwise, I was just conceited. And every "good" woman knows there's nothing worse than being selfish and conceited. Except maybe being a slut or a prude, depending on the conversation taking place behind your back, but that's a whole other book.

My hopes of external validation often went unfulfilled because it turns out no one except for me knew I needed it. I was naïve and thought that everyone lived this way. When I saw someone getting complimented, I thought, *Oh nice, they see her and complimented her so she now knows she's good enough to take the next steps in life. They see her worth.* And then the compliments passed by, skipping me completely, so obviously I thought I should rot in hell with the other cockroaches of society.

That day in a crowded, loud, disgusting Subway booth, this man had gruffly pointed out that I needed to stop constantly looking to others for direction and validation. I'm still so grateful for this candid conversation. Because since then I've come to learn that listening too much to others can set you off course and keep you off course for quite some time.

When you're brought up to be "good" and follow the rules, staying on the course set by others can feel easy and simple—like a no-brainer. You know exactly what to do. But if you sit down and really pay attention, you'll see that following the rules of others for too long will slowly eat you alive until you're an unfulfilled husk of a human.

I wasn't looking for a mentor because I was forging my own path. I was looking for a mentor because I needed validation. Once I realized I was looking for a pat on the head to let me know I was still headed in the right direction—and on a course that wasn't even mine, no less—I knew things had to change.

This conversation, and the embarrassing realization that I was a validation-seeking-attention-whore, helped catapult me into a new space. I decided to pay more attention to those around me and how they assessed their worth, their successes, their weaknesses. No one is perfect, but people still have amazing lives. How do they do that? How do they know what they are good at? How do they know which path to take? It was time to take a breather from all of that rule following, look up, and look around.

And guess what? Unfortunately, I didn't have an epiphany or anything even remotely helpful. Because I was still looking to others! I was watching so I could secretly get validation from them without them even knowing. Once I caught myself doing this, I was even more confused. So, where the heck was I supposed to go next on my journey? Where should I direct my feet if I'm supposed to think for myself and not follow the well-worn path?

There were no signs, no directions. *No validation.* And no one popped up out of the ground like a fairy godmother to confirm that this was actually what I should be doing.

In fact, it felt like the opposite, like I was so lost that I should stay on that well-worn, familiar path that wasn't even the correct path for me. My default assessment of myself was that I sucked. At everything. So maybe I should get back on that already-paved path and keep my mouth shut and my head down.

Thankfully, I knew deep down there was no way I actually sucked. I had a job, I paid my bills, I had friends, I had happy kids—there was no way I was as bad at life as my bully brain made me out to be.

Because of that, I decided that I just had to choose to be brave and learn as I go. Learning as you go takes a lot of self-forgiveness. I had to take a good look at myself *on my own.* I had to find my own truth.

Be Honest with Yourself and Celebrate Your Sparkles

There are a lot of articles and books out there about how to be honest with yourself. Those articles will ask you to *honestly* look at your faults and mistakes and work on fixing them. Which is great advice! But what about those of us *who only focus on our faults*? We know *all about our faults*—it's all we think about. I want you to take a different approach. I want you to take an honest look at your *strengths*. Write them down and celebrate them.

When I first started this, I had such a hard time listing what I was good at. The first thing I ever wrote down was, "I'm weird," and I celebrated that.

This exercise stuck with me *for months*. It started with me looking at a blank piece of paper and thinking, "OMG, what if I'm not good at anything?!" and then realizing being weird is a good trait. It draws other weird people to me and we help each other get through life. Writing down just one thing was what I needed to get started on this activity.

The question "What am I good at?" stayed in the back of my mind for a really long time and I still have it sitting back there. I don't want to miss out on noticing something I'm good at! Slowly, I started to see more and more things pop up. For example, did you know that I'm really good at working with female business owners and helping them feel confident in moving forward with marketing plans that will make them highly visible in the marketplace? Female business owners deal with a lot more bullshit than men do all day, and being front and center in their industry can be scary. By paying attention to meetings that went well, to feedback from clients, and how I felt after interactions with others, I found out that I'm freaking awesome at helping them create plans for moving forward and even plans for what to do if their worst fears happen.

It's time to start your own list. What makes you sparkle? Either to yourself or to others? I promise, you do sparkle. There are many personality tests out there and feel free to use those later. For now, I want you to take your own assessment. To get past any mental blocks that come with complimenting yourself, I've created a list of questions that'll help you create a bigger picture of your life. You'll start to see things you enjoy and what you're good at as you follow along!

Find Your Happy Place

Take three minutes to close your eyes and picture yourself at peace, feeling carefree with no obligations weighing you down.

- Where are you?
- What are you looking at?
- What are you doing?
- What do you smell?
- What are you standing on?
- What are you wearing?
- Who are you with?
- What do you hear?
- What is making you feel like this is your happy place?

Open your eyes and write it all down. Try to include all of your senses.

Find Your Heart Connections

Next step, take three minutes again to close your eyes and picture yourself hanging out with others and having a blast.

- What are you doing?
- What are you talking about?
- What makes you laugh?
- What makes you feel like you're with people who love you?
- What makes you think "I want to do this again soon?"

Open your eyes and write it all down.

Find Your Money-Maker

Time to close your eyes again. Take three minutes to think about your current job. Yes, even if you hate it. Think about these next answers while assessing the tasks, the discussions, and the people you work with. Not your actual job. You're working towards happiness and fulfillment, so focus on the good things at work.

- When did you smile at your job?
- When did you receive positive feedback from anyone there (not just managers)?
- When did you feel successful?
- When did you feel like you were contributing?
- When did you bring a positive story home to tell a friend, partner, or family member?

Open your eyes and write it all down.

Hype Yourself Up

It's time to make a list of what you're good at. You've spent time thinking about your happy place, your connections, and your job. Each of those three scenarios you spent three minutes thinking about will help you with this. Look at what you have written down.

- What personality traits and strengths have helped you get those moments?
- Are you curious, responsible, adventurous, loyal, friendly, innovative, brave, humorous?
- Are you good at cooking, storytelling, rock climbing, teaching others, math?
- Are you easy-going, artistic, realistic, clever, romantic, perceptive?
- Which of your traits fit into your happy place, your heart connections, and your money-making worlds?

Ask Others

Next, start asking others to help you build your list. Start with family and friends who love you. You can ask them what strengths you have, why they like hanging out with you, and what they admire about you. You can also ask co-workers and past managers what strengths they see in you. This is not the time to ask for "constructive" feedback. No, ma'am, you only want to know about the good things. What are your strengths? If you don't think the person can do that for you, then leave them off the list of people you're going to ask.

Keep Building Your List

Going forward, promise yourself that you're going to keep adding to the list. When you're feeling down or like an imposter out there navigating the high-winds and storms, you can come back to your list for a reality check. Because this is the true reality you need to keep coming back to.

Meditate on Your List

In the morning, get your list out. Place it in front of you and take the time to read the entire thing. Play meditative music if you want. If your mornings are rushed, then maybe just write them on a sticky note and post it in your bathroom so you can read the list while you brush your teeth. Either way, keep reminding yourself daily about your strengths. There will be a point in the future when someone will try to belittle you and you're going to be pleasantly surprised when your first reaction is "that's not true" because you *know* who you are. You've been reminding yourself daily.

This exercise builds your own validation, so you have the internal fortitude needed to create your own path. You no longer need to follow paths created by others. Especially as you go back and look through your Sparkles list. How could you follow someone else's path when you're so different and you have so many wonderful attributes to utilize?!

Boost Confidence with Mirror Work

Mirrors are magical on their own—captivating civilizations throughout history, often symbolizing introspection, truth, and even the supernatural. From reflecting your inner goddess back to you to unveiling hidden truths that you couldn't see before, the use of mirrors hasn't always been just about doing our hair or wishing we looked different naked.

This activity invites you to make a connection between the tangible and the intangible and see a mirror beyond its utilitarian purpose. You're going to use it as a portal to self-discovery that reflects your own feelings and subconscious back to you.

Mirror work consists of looking directly at yourself in the mirror and hyping yourself up. Initially, you can feel a bit silly, like you're hosting a one-person comedy show in the privacy of your bathroom. The first few attempts might make you feel self-conscious and awkward. But I encourage you to stick with it. Remember, the only audience member witnessing your self-affirming spectacle is the person who matters most—you. So, stand tall, laugh off the initial silliness, and let your bathroom mirror become the safe space where confidence takes center stage.

There are two levels to mirror work:

1. Staring at your face in the mirror while stating affirmations and complimenting yourself.

2. Stripping down to appreciate your body and complimenting yourself. This is level two for a reason! It can take months or even years to get here. Don't burn this book. Just start at level one.

Mirror work is designed to help you learn to love yourself and the world around you, which is paramount while embarking on the journey of building your own path in life.

Replace External Validations with Internal Knowledge

Replacing external validations with internal knowledge means you need to start trusting yourself more. This mirror work activity will help you build compassion, confidence, and trust with yourself. Mirror work is called *work* for a reason. It takes time, but the journey is worth the results.

Here are some directions on how to perform mirror work:

Find a Quiet and Comfortable Space

Look for a private space where you can be alone and have uninterrupted time for mirror work. It can be a room, a bathroom, or any area where you can easily see yourself in a mirror.

Set the Right Atmosphere

If you're just getting started, I recommend creating a calming and positive safe space. You can dim the lights, light some candles, or play soft, uplifting music to set a peaceful ambience.

If you've graduated to more intense mirror work, where you're stripping down, then I'd recommend music that makes you feel sexy or confident.

Stand in Front of a Mirror

Stand directly in front of a mirror so that you can see your entire reflection, or at least your face.

Make Eye Contact with Yourself

Look into your own eyes in the mirror. Allow yourself to connect with your reflection and be present in the moment. If you're conducting the more intense version of mirror work, then go ahead and look at your body, too.

This may feel uncomfortable at first but stay with it.

Start With Positive Affirmation

Begin by repeating positive affirmations to yourself out loud. Choose affirmations that resonate with you and focus on building your self-confidence.

- "I am confident and capable."
- "I love and accept myself unconditionally."
- "I am deserving of success and happiness."

Use positive and encouraging words. Avoid criticizing or judging yourself. Remember, the goal is to build self-confidence, so be compassionate and supportive. If you're looking at your entire body, you might want to say, "Ugh gross," like you usually do. Refrain from it. If you can't compliment your body, then at least hold judgment back.

Express Gratitude for Yourself

Take a moment to express gratitude for who you are and what you have accomplished. Recognize the challenges you have overcome and the growth you have. Tell yourself "Thank you" out loud.

If you're standing in front of your mirror naked and trying your hardest to hold back judgment, then you've already taken a huge step. Now it's time to thank your body for what it does for you. Do your arms hold people you love closer to you? Say thank you. Do your legs take you on fabulous walks at sunset? Say thank you. Does your tummy digest food so you can have the nutrients you need to survive? Say thank you. Do your stretch marks mean that you were healthy enough to grow up and grow out? Say thank you. Does your skin have nerve endings that allow you to feel pleasure? Say thank you.

Practice Self-Love and Acceptance

Embrace and accept yourself fully, including your perceived flaws and imperfections. The thing is, your body does so much for you. It lets you find pleasure in food, in feeling the sun on your face, in feeling your muscles stretch and strengthen when you're active, in feeling pleasure in the bedroom. It does all of this for you. Even while you say horribly negative things about it. While you look on in disgust, it's been working hard to give you pleasure in life. It's time to see it for what it really is and say, "Thank you." And not just "Thank you" but "Thank you, you sexy bitch."

Treat yourself with love, respect, and kindness throughout the mirror work session. Aim to perform this exercise daily, or at least a few times a week.

I give you permission to sit back and treat yourself like a goddess. Let your subjects tell you all the wonderful things about you. Bask in the glory. Agree with them. Yes, you are that good! And yes, you are going to forge new paths based on all of those jaw-dropping, awe-inspiring talents that you possess.

I AM ENOUGH. EVERYTHING I NEED IS INSIDE OF ME.

5. HANDING SHAME BACK

"No, thanks."

It's time to start saying stupid shit like "no shame in my game" but actually mean it.

Wanna read something fucked up? Then keep reading, I gotchu.

But first, an introduction to shame.

People-pleasing. Perfectionism. Addictions. Excessive behaviors. Low self-worth. Exhaustion. Depression. Feeling flawed. Being defensive. Anxious 24/7.

Shame is a feeling that sits at the core of many of us.

Women are raised with shame as one of their first companions. We are brought up to sit lady like, our emotions are bad, our bodies are bad, our voices are bad, our periods are disgusting and shouldn't be talked about, we have to hide our boobs if we get them "too young," we're not the right height if we're taller than men, our bodies are disappointing unless we look airbrushed, shit... just not being white and blonde. Add in the sexual traumas that most of us experience and we're steeped in piping hot, steaming shame from a young age.

We're Stuck Inside Our Bodies

This shame is woven into our skin. Like an internal straight jacket. It's constricting our entire world, narrowing our viewpoints down to just our own bodies. Shame squeezes our hearts, fighting love and growth and worthiness. Shame constricts our vocal cords until we choke.

Shame leaves a mark on your body and your consciousness each time it invades your space. It grows stronger each day by gobbling up your goals, your relationships, and your *health*.

Shame makes you feel like you're constantly doing something wrong. That you are wrong, and your existence is wrong. *It stops you from trusting yourself.*

Now for the fucked-up part, as promised.

I'm addicted to feeling shame. That horrible feeling that floods my organs, bones, and muscles with a rush of energy, like my blood might burst from my arteries at any moment. That feeling of being frozen in place, while my insides move at warp speed with disappointment and regret and sadness, is familiar to my brain and body. It's why I procrastinate so much. Procrastination, perfectionism, and other self-sabotaging behaviors are a very efficient way to place those feelings back into my body.

If I can't get the feeling of shame from another place, then I'll procrastinate and find a way to hate myself for the rest of the day that way.

I was so used to the constant shame in my life that I didn't realize I could *or should* feel differently. It was my normal. And when I moved away from that normal, I'd self-sabotage to ensure I moved back to my comfort zone—my comfort zone of feeling like complete dog shit and hating myself.

It wasn't until I was in my thirties that I realized shame followed me after anything happened in my life. Good or bad. It was always there. Make a mistake? Shame. Accomplish a goal? Shame. Always shame. And it wasn't until just a few years ago that I realized I was completely addicted to these feelings and that I was finding ways to reset myself back to those feelings.

Not everyone is a shame junkie like me. But we all fight the hold it has on us.

Shame Came from Outside of Us

Where do these feelings of shame come from? It comes from the outside of our bodies as we grow up. It comes from the abuses we endure—physical, mental, emotional, sexual. Each manipulation and abuse brings a cloud of shame that first sits over our heads and then lowers down to settle into our hips, anchoring us to a place of constant discomfort. It creates sickness and body aches and pains.

It might come from the outside, but once it's in your body. It wants to stay there forever.

Shame and trauma will stay in your body unless you force it out. It shows up slowly, affecting your immune system, endocrine system, autonomic nervous system, sleep/wake cycle, and can even cause eating disorders. Not to mention causing dissociation, feelings of helplessness and despair, anxiety, mood swings, and obsessive-compulsive thoughts.

It's filling your body full of disease.

If shame originally comes from the outside and it's not ours to begin with, then why are we the ones stuck with it? And how the hell do we get rid of it?!

Through lots of work, babe.

Dig into Your Past to Release Shame

Releasing your shame is a messy, emotional process, but it's 100 percent worth it.

It all starts by digging into your past—don't close the book yet! Keep reading. I promise there are ways to do this without getting swallowed up by the shadows of your past.

Feeling like a baby deer frozen under the tractor beams of some asshole's headlights on a dark rural road is a sensation that we're used to. Moving out of the frozen Bambi state into a villainous goddess is a big step. How do you go from terrified prey to a goddess wielding a sword of truth and protection?

By removing shame.

Acknowledging these feelings stuck in your body and giving them a way out is essential at this stage of healing and to villain era survival. You will be a new person after this!

There are plenty of support tools out there ready to help you navigate this journey. Do this with the help of a professional or with books that outline the tools you need to help you process whatever memories come up.

I liked *Happy Days: The Guided Path from Trauma to Profound Freedom and Inner Peace* by Gabby Berstein. She has spent thousands of dollars in therapy and outlined the tools that she's used with many of her therapists.

Tools like "body work" which includes the emotional freedom technique, also known as EFT (like tapping) and meditation. I used tapping, meditation, and guided journaling to help with processing my memories.

Inner child work is essential during this phase as well. I also took an "Inner Bonding" course (innerbonding.com) that's designed to help you look at your childhood and how you were raised and heal your inner child. This was the first eye opening experience for me, and it helped me start researching other therapies to try.

There are many books out there to help you get started. Read the reviews to make sure it's a book that you'll connect with and then dig in!

Guided meditations are excellent as well. You can get a list of meditations, YouTube videos, and books I've found helpful at VillainEraGoddess.com.

Next, it's time to start identifying your triggers and accepting that you have them. This will help you transition into the next stage and have more control as you heal. Whenever you feel triggered, start journaling about what happened, how it made you feel, and keep journaling... and keep journaling.

Keep looking closer and closer at your emotions. Do you feel ashamed? Why? Write that down. Do you feel anger? Why? Write that down.

This has helped me uncover memories. It's also helped me see how I react to triggers so I can learn to soothe and comfort myself versus reacting negatively. If you're not sure what your triggers are, then just journal whenever you have very strong emotions about something. You'll eventually see a pattern emerge. And that, my dear, is your trigger.

I really liked the "rage on a page" journal exercise in Gabby Bernstein's book *Happy Days*. It allowed me to get to every single emotion—from the huge emotions I knew I was feeling to the hidden emotions underneath that I didn't know were there, too. This has been one of the most effective techniques for me and has unlocked many memories and helped me see patterns in my family and in myself.

Make sure you know what support tools you're going to use (meditation, tapping, journaling, etc.) so you're not out there without your armor.

The Memories Are Horrible, But You're Not

Uncovering trauma and old memories is a horrible process. You may be thinking that you don't want to remember anything that might add to the anxiety, anger, disappointment, and sadness to your already busy, stressful life.

You might not want to shine a spotlight on the truth of past abuses while also trying to navigate everyday life and everything that comes with it.

You might not want anymore bullshit because they're already *exhausted.* This is when I get questions like, "But exactly how did you do it?" and "How did you get through it?"

You might be looking for reassurances that it won't be that bad before you start taking a close look at your fears. Babe, there aren't any. There are absolutely no reassurances. You have to be ready to heal—no matter what you face—so you can live a better life.

But I can tell you this…

It all comes back to your quality of life. Do you want to be *exactly where you are right now* for the rest of your life?

Do you want the same feelings of unworthiness, constant anxiety, stomach issues, memory issues, and chronic illness that you have right now?

Do you want to feel unworthy of money, unworthy of love, or unworthy of attention and compliments?

I'm assuming the answer is no. If you have your tools ready, then I fully believe it's going to be easier than what you're imagining. I had moments after an old traumatic memory was uncovered where I just sat there by myself, numb. Not even processing it yet. Just numb. Then I'd move into processing it because I didn't want any of those memories or feelings to be stuck in my body because I ignored them. I was doing this hard work so my quality of life would be better. And I made the decision to be dedicated to the cause.

Ritual to Reclaim Your Body

I believe that each time shame settles into your body, it replaces a piece of you. That piece is with the person who took it from you or left in the location where it was taken from you.

A vital piece of you was removed. The wholesome energy that lives in your skin, your muscles and bone, and all of your organs, was stolen. It's time to take them back.

The following activity helps you call those pieces back to you so you can become whole again. I think there's a reason why different religions and spiritual practices have rituals that call pieces of yourself and your soul back to you. Because we instinctively know pieces of ourselves get scattered in this messy life.

Start in a quiet space where you won't be disturbed.

Materials Needed:
- Candles (white or any color that resonates with you)
- Incense or dried herbs for cleansing
- Relaxing music
- Crystals (such as rose quartz for love, amethyst for healing, and clear quartz for clarity)

Preparation:
- Choose a time and space where you won't be disturbed.
- Cleanse the space by lighting incense or dried herbs, allowing the smoke to purify your environment.
- Set up your candles, crystals, and symbolic objects in front of you.
- Play relaxing music if you'd like help creating a more calming atmosphere.

Reclaim yourself:

1. Open your energy. Hold out your hands or lift up your arms like you're receiving something and say, "I reclaim my energy. Any parts of me that have been removed from trauma, stress, and the daily burdens of life are to come back to me now."

2. Leave your hands or arms open and take deep, meditative breaths.

3. Imagine light filling your body, making you a beacon in the storm. The pieces of you will see the beacon and be called home.

4. Visualize the pieces of you returning home. Welcome them and tell them you love them.

5. Feel all the feelings that come with being reunited with love and home.

6. Recite affirmations that resonate with you, affirming your intention to become whole again. For example: "I am reclaiming my power," "I am healing and integrating," or "I am whole and complete."

The first time I called pieces of myself back to me, I bawled. I did this ritual in the bathtub and with each piece that came back to me, a memory or feeling came with it—of how I came about missing that piece. I was left with a lot of rage, but most importantly, I was left with relief and the feeling of being one step closer to being healed. This is a wonderful way to take back your control as you move forward.

Live Outside of Your Body

I said earlier that shame keeps us stuck inside our bodies. When we start releasing shame, we start to actually *live*.

We're more likely to live in the moment and notice more things around us that we can enjoy. We notice other body sensations—fun ones! Like the sunshine warming the side of your face while driving. Or the breeze that lifts your hair and rearranges it in a more "natural" look. Or how soft your carpet is after you vacuum. We notice so much more.

I give you permission to let go of that tricky bitch known as shame. Shame isn't even her real name. She's a memory, emotion, or trigger dressed in an ugly beige dress to disguise herself. We don't accept imposters and you're going to kick her to the curb.

I FEEL GOOD.
I AM GOOD.
I CREATE GOOD.

6. NO IS A VIBE

Stop being agreeable and start screaming "no."

Let's play a game. Count how many people make you feel like an asshole after reading this chapter.

Saying "no" can literally save you and your family. I promise I'm not being dramatic. Being agreeable 100 percent of the time can lead to worse things than just burnout, resentment, and a lack of fulfillment in life. It can lead to self-loathing, unsafe situations, and unconscious support of abusers in your family and social group.

Groomed Into Being a "Giver"

If you grew up in a household where big emotions weren't handled well by adults, then I bet nowadays everyone describes you as a very "pleasant" person to be around.

Finding yourself unable to say "no" is not a character flaw you were born with. It's a result of your childhood. It could be from having parents who made you feel like you had to conform or perform to "earn" their affection. From overly strict parents. Emotionally unstable parents. And even from a strict religious upbringing.

Add your childhood experiences to the fact that women are just expected to be polite, nurturing, and agreeable all the fucking time—even at the expense of their own well-being—and you've just been handed a "doormat" cocktail full of depression and anxiety.

When I talk about being agreeable and saying yes to everything, I'm not just talking about declining outrageous requests like, "Will you take me to the airport at 3:00 a.m.?" I'm talking about how you show up in life.

It's time to weave a thick, heavy cloak of "*I think the fuck not*" around yourself so people know to approach you respectfully. Using your "no" vibe to ensure you're treated like a real person with real goals and feelings who won't be sacrificed for others any longer. I'm not telling you to be a bitch (but, please be a bitch if you need to). I'm telling you to hold yourself differently, so you're approached in a manner that means you have the final say.

Don't Seek Support, Just Set the Boundaries

When I first started thinking about setting boundaries around the abusers in my family, I realized just how much of an uphill battle was in front of me. Even the people who weren't abusers or power-hungry manipulators were used to having the final say in how I responded to them.

I still remember one of the most overwhelming mornings I've ever had when I started building boundaries. This isn't even a dramatic story of an abuser trying to gain access to me. No, it was from a family member I love. I was in my bathrobe, trying to enjoy my first cup of coffee in the morning and a self-help book.

I sat outside on the patio with the birds chirping, the sun warming up the right half of my body, the shade cooling the left side of my body, and my little fur-baby on my lap. I was enjoying my relaxing morning routine as I prepared myself for the day. I had started my own business and was in the "grow as fast as you can" stage so I could pay my bills without going into debt (you entrepreneurs know exactly what stage I'm talking about).

My beloved family member sent me a text message asking if I could go shopping with her that afternoon. I let her know that I couldn't because I had a lot of work to get done that day and since this was a last-minute invite, I didn't work ahead to account for the time I'd be taking off.

The response was pure chaos. Text after text of guilt-ridden messages of not prioritizing family, shame-inducing messages like I wasn't smart enough to find a solution to getting my work done... while skipping work to go hang out. More guilt about how it was the only time she could see me for the next week. I was so overwhelmed. If this person went straight to being condescending and couldn't respectfully support my answer of just not hanging out for the afternoon, was she going to support me later when it was time to say "no" to the big stuff?

This was small potatoes compared to the big fully flavored meal of boundaries I was getting ready to serve piping hot. What would happen when I had to stand up and say "no" to the big, scary stuff?

In the past I would have relented, went shopping for the afternoon, and then stayed up until midnight after my kids were in bed to make up the work I was supposed to finish that day. And honestly, that would have been easier than dealing with text after text of condescending insults, but wouldn't have been the right move for my long-term boundary setting plans.

The realization of just how alone I was on this journey turned into a dark, heavy cloud of anxiety that covered my entire body. I felt truly alone. The person who I thought would fully support me had blown up over something small. How the hell was I going to do this without her support?

Saying "No" is Ugly Work but Worth It

I realized I was going to upset *everyone*, even those I thought would have my back. I had morphed into an even-bigger villain.

As I started saying "no" more and more, I was met with more and more shocked, livid people. I was always counted on to say "yes" every single time. Nobody was happy about me standing up for myself. No one shouted "You go, girl" like we were in a cheesy '90s movie. Not one person supported me. Because the people I was saying "no" to were the ones who had already planned their lives around my "yes." Their day was planned around me being agreeable and helpful.

This part sucks—the beginning of your villain era when you're saying "no" and dealing with the fall-out. I wanted to wear a shirt 24/7 that said, "Really? Has no one ever said 'no' to you fuckers before?" But I felt like that might have been too aggressive and probably offensive to elderly folks at the grocery store.

I kept saying "no" and I kept dealing with the aftermath. And I'm sorry to say to my dear readers, this part didn't get better for quite some time. Their anger escalated when I started saying "no" to bigger things. I said "no" to seeing family members who came from out-of-town. I "let my family down" by not putting family first. If I had a dime for every time I heard "Well, I'm just sad that you don't care about staying in touch with family" then I'd have at least twenty bucks. Little did they know I *was* putting my family first—me and my kids.

I can attest that it takes years of being a villain before the majority of the folks get the message. Especially if you don't have anyone backing you up. I had no one backing me up for almost a decade. And unfortunately, it took a news article featuring the horrific things a family member did to an underage girl to make my family take notice and listen to me. It was hard, and I believe it would have continued to be a horrible struggle if that news article hadn't come out.

When and Why to Say "No"

After re-writing your "Acceptable and Good" list from chapter two, you'll have a better idea of when you need to say "no" in order to protect yourself and your family. No one knows your limits, values, goals, and history like you do. So no one else gets a say in when and how you say no.

Good times to say no are when:
- you feel uncomfortable
- you feel guilty or obligated
- you have too much going on and you can't take anymore at the moment
- your boundaries will be crossed when you say yes

You'll learn to identify signs of discomfort in your body and listen to your body more often as you set boundaries and keep saying no.

How to Say No Like a True Villainous Queen

There are many articles and books you can read about how to say no when the time comes. And we'll cover a few soon. But first I want to talk about "how," as in how you *present* the "no," not necessarily the words you use.

As you first start saying "no" you *might not* be proud of how you handle it. The one thing I want you to remember from this chapter is that the whole point is you following through with saying no. It's not the words you use. It's not whether you cried or screamed (I've done both) while saying no. It's not how offended the other person was. It has nothing to do with if they understood what you were trying to say (hint: they never will). It's that you did it. You said no.

Here's why those things don't matter: You're a doormat in recovery. You instinctually work to not offend someone. So, if you scream, cry, and get offensive then it was time to behave that way and it's ok. So do not worry about how you presented the no and focus on the fact that it's time to say no and be proud of yourself for doing it. It won't always be that way, so give yourself grace and patience here. And please remember, you are a wonderful person, you're not the asshole here.

I'm all for the direct approaches to saying no, and I agree that is the healthier approach. But we all know that one fucker who will argue with you non-stop and keep throwing guilt at you. What do you do with that person? Well, I've been told that it's not appropriate to kick them in their scrunched up, condescending faces. So, I guess we have to use our words.

One of the most important things to remember while you're laying a floor of "no" tiles in the entryway of your villainous castle is that you are just as important as everyone else. Your comfort is just as important as anyone else's.

I had to learn this and then remind myself over and over. If I ask "is person x going to be there because last time they did some unhinged shit" then I have every right to ask that. If the person asking me to come over treats me like I'm the problem, then I have every right to remind them I'm just as important.

Saying "no" can be difficult at first. There are many ways to say "no" and it can depend on the situation. If you're struggling to find the words, then start with this list below. Soon you'll be slinging no's around like you've done it your whole life!

<u>A light and simple no</u>
- "No, thank you. I won't be able to."
- "Thank you for asking, but I can't make it."
- "I can't, but did you ask so and so? They are into that."
- "Oh shoot, if you would have asked sooner, I would have said yes. But I already have plans."
- "I'm grateful you asked, but I can't at this time."

- "I can't do that. But here is what I can do . . . "

When I know there's a fight coming and I want to avoid it

- "I'll get back to you. I have a calendar at home I need to look at or I need to ask [person] if we're busy or not." Then send a text later saying no.
- "Sounds horrible. Last time [insert exactly what bothered you]. But I guess I'll think about if I can stomach it or not. I'll text you later."

I've started listing the specific reason why

- "After [person] did [action] last time, I promised myself I'd never sit through something like that again. I'm not going to be able to make it."
- "I have three days off work to celebrate this holiday, I just can't dedicate that time to suffering through [persons name] or [situation]."

When the guilt comes

- "I don't want to spend my time with people who [call out the behavior]. Good for you that you can ignore it and it doesn't bother you. My family finds that type of behavior very unacceptable and we no longer want to witness it."
- "If you really do want to hang out with me and my family, then we need to do it in a way that works for us, too. Let's talk about other ideas."
- "If you're open later and you really do want to see me then you can come to my house on a different day."
- "I'm hurt that you're pressuring me. I was hoping you'd want to see my side of this, too."
- "I have diarrhea!" and either hang up the phone or run away from them (not recommended if there's a lot of witnesses).

<u>Get honest about why you're saying no</u>
- "I'm trying to be truthful with you instead of lying or ghosting you."
- "I want to keep you in my life, so I need to set this boundary."
- "I've always wanted to set this boundary but was scared you'd react exactly like how you're reacting."

I also like to plan ahead. I've left family events and texted my mom saying, "Please remember [insert situation] because when I say 'no' next year, this is exactly why," and it works. She was still feeling the impact of the dramatic situation and understood. She didn't say a word the following year. In fact, she stuck up for me when people asked where my family was.

You're Doing It Right—Even If It Feels Too Hard

It's important to keep in mind that setting boundaries can be pretty ugly at first. Especially if your "proof" is in the gray area. If you don't have a news article and you only have stories from cousins, patterns of behaviors you've witnessed, and nothing that's "good enough" for the rest of your family members, then your road will be filled with all sorts of people who would absolutely love to cast the first stone. And after you say "no" you won't always feel relief. In fact, you probably will rarely feel relief during the beginning of your villain era. Especially if you're still recovering from the conditioning of being a doormat.

Standing up to say what you want when you know that no one cares what you want is like staring your worst nightmare right in the face, breathing its bad breath, watching it bare its teeth. It's like getting on your hands and knees to check to see if the monster under your bed is still there and seeing that, yes, it's still freaking there.

When you get to this phase—where you're staring the monster in the face—it's important to remember why you're in your villain era and why you're saying no. Nothing puts the "fight" back into your body faster than being reminded of what you're protecting.

Remember Why You're Doing This

"No" allows you to take ownership of your own life and make decisions that align with your values and goals. You already know that society, abusers, and others are more comfortable with their foot on your neck.

"No" quickly sets boundaries and helps you break free so you can stand up and brush yourself off.

Saying "no" is so hard. Actually, calling it "hard" is an understatement. Taking a stand when you know you're on your own *is terrifying*. The only way I've found to make it easier on myself is to remember why I'm doing it.

Whether it's for you or your children, you have decided that you and your family come first. When you keep focusing on that, it becomes easier to say "no." In the beginning, I would focus on my kids (because I was still working on self-worth) and I would remind myself that they are worth more than anyone else in my family. I choose them every time. I choose them over everything and everyone.

You can't backslide when you remind yourself of the why.

I now know that I'm worth it, too. I also choose *me* over everyone else in my family. *Me*. I'm worth it. I'm worth the uncomfortable discussions, the rude replies from family, the condescending tones. I'm totally worth the effort to stand up and say, "You fuck around and you find out."

Write down why you're in your villain era. Why you have the right to say NO.

- Who are you protecting?

- What (or who) are you protecting them against?
- What values are you upholding? Here are examples of mine:
    - We respect each other and our boundaries
    - We strive for open communication and listening
    - We always believe each other's stories
    - We offer support during times of need
    - We share responsibilities and help out
    - We foster a sense of belonging and acceptance
    - We are diligent about security and safety
    - We offer compassion and forgiveness while growing
    - We create a safe environment to learn and grow

Use this as your reminder when you face the unpleased masses of people who haven't yet figured out that their opinion doesn't matter anymore.

Don't forget, you were only praised for being "good" and putting others first. You were probably scolded for "being selfish" when you put yourself first. It's normal for this phase to feel uncomfortable.

Saying "no" and refusing to be agreeable helps us shake off societal expectations and build boundaries. It's the dirty work necessary to take control of our lives. When women are unable to set boundaries and communicate their needs effectively, they struggle to build healthy relationships with everyone in their lives. It's often how we find ourselves in toxic relationships. Don't skip this important step!

👑 *I give you permission to be the biggest fucking bitch you can image. I give you permission to leave these folks speechless. I want them sitting there with their mouths open. I want them not able to blink. I give you permission to choose yourself over everyone else. I know you're a loving, caring person and you do so much for those you love. I'm asking you to stop sacrificing yourself for everyone else.*

I SAY "YES" TO PEACE, LOVE AND SAFETY.

7. VICTIM TO VILLAIN

Shed the victim label like a snakeskin.

You can lie down and play dead or you can get up and live.

Before we move on in the book, I need to say something that's going to make your skin feel like it's wrapped too tightly around your bones. It's going to make your stomach rise into your throat until it hurts to breathe. You might want to shove this book down your garbage disposal after reading this chapter.

Playing the victim role feels good. I'm not saying that *being* victimized feels good and I'm not saying that you deserve anything that happened to you. So read this again. *Playing* the victim feels good. It comes with the high of a validation we've been seeking since we were kids. It comes with guaranteed sympathy, guaranteed kindness, guaranteed that someone is going to listen to your story and feel bad for you. Someone is going to agree that yes, you are a victim, and yes, your life was bad. They will agree that yes, you can't stop bad people from doing bad things. And yes, that should have never happened to you. And most importantly, yes, you really were a victim in that scenario.

If you're not careful, it can come with the permission your tired self needs to stop trying to heal, to curl in on yourself and hide. It's lying down to play dead like playing dead is a reward.

The ironic thing is that when we were children and needed that validation and to be cared for, many of us didn't get it. Now as adults, we might crave validation for our victimization to the point of this craving getting in our way of growing and healing. We've been waiting for others to acknowledge our pain our whole lives! Of course, we're going to jump at this opportunity, push others off the stage, and hog the spotlight.

Sympathy can feel like guaranteed kindness. Which is why you have to be careful. What starts as taking comfort from someone can lead you to tap-dancing across the damn stage for more spotlight. I should know. I've been there in my tap shoes. Apparently, I carry tap shoes in my purse, because this issue repeatedly comes up in my healing journey.

Let me tell you about the time the spotlight was moved off my interpretive dance number titled "The Woes of Ashley" and instead shined into my heart and onto my intentions. For the first time ever in my life, I met a person I couldn't get enough of. I loved him down to his bone marrow, down to the mitochondria of his cells. This man, who looked like he was carved from the temples of Angkor Wat with brown eyes that glowed with an orange fire from within, looked over at me and I was *done*.

Fast forward to our first big argument. He told me he wasn't sure if I was a good fit for him because, based on my past relationships, it looked like I had a pattern of choosing the wrong people to date. And he would know because I had just finished a dance performance titled "How My Exes Ruined My Life" while trying to hog more spotlight. He didn't know if I was choosing him because I truly wanted him or because I was still stuck in a self-sabotage mindset and choosing him because he fit some pattern based on my unhealed wounds.

What! Ok, sir. The audacity to take my victimhood away from me! I had never been *so called out in my fucking life*. It was the biggest slap in the face I'd ever felt. Because he was right, damn it, and it was 100 percent the healthiest move he could make to *protect himself* from *me*.

As you can imagine, I didn't handle it well. I remember sobbing and being so pissed at him because he was right. And then I was pissed at myself because he was right. And then I was pissed at the entire world because *he was right.*

I did need to slow down and make sure I was approaching my relationship with him with pure intentions. That I was not letting my wounded inner child make hasty decisions that would hurt both of us in the end.

And honestly, I was embarrassed he had to call that out.

This was when I started paying more attention to where I wanted to be in my healing journey. Did I want to continue being the victim? The answer came from the bottom of my feet, through my legs, through my stomach, up my throat as a loud "No!"

It was time to work on healing. Like *really* healing. To make a commitment to stop being the victim.

Please seriously consider that you may need to take this step, too. How much better would you feel if you weren't the victim anymore? If you picked up this book, then I truly believe that you're at a point in your life where you're done laying down and letting everyone inspect your wounds.

Instead, you're going to stand up, brush yourself off, pull out your wedgie, and give yourself the love and attention you seek. You're going to implement daily routines to continue to care for yourself and protect yourself while healing. We'll do it together!

I give you permission to call your own ass out. Put your tap shoes away and forget about your DIY theater performances. Your life isn't about what happened to you. Your life is about learning, loving, and LIVING. You're scarier than the skeletons in the closet. You're more terrifying than the monsters under the bed. What do you say? Make this the time you get up and act like the Goddess you are.

I'M NOT A VICTIM. I'M A VILLAINOUS GODDESS AND I OWN MY WORTH.

REBUILDING YOURSELF IN THIS NEW ERA

8. YOU'RE NOT BROKEN

But you do need to heal.

Honey, it's not your fault. You grew up enduring trauma.

I grew up with mysterious stomach issues that would leave my body wracked with pain. I had memory issues, learning issues, chronic pain in my body, and no idea why. I would go to the doctor once a year getting lab work full of blood samples so they could tell me that nothing was wrong with me. *Over twenty years of this!*

Then I finally stumbled upon information regarding trauma and chronic fear and what it does to your body and your brain. And. Let. Me. Tell. You. I was pissed! Turns out my body wasn't broken because I was defective. It was exhausted and overstimulated by fear and trauma. All of this was because I grew up experiencing unsafe situations.

Being raised in an environment that kept you in a constant state of alert and fear warped your growing brain and changed it before you even got a chance at life. Your need to always read facial expressions, body language, people in the room, and stay alert puts you behind others at the start line in the rat race we call life.

The connection between the mind and body is a powerful one, and understanding how trauma manifests physically can help you navigate the healing process more effectively. Your body stores your trauma and unless you force it out, it affects your

- immune system
- endocrine system
- autonomic nervous system
- sleep/wake cycle

Not to mention it can cause eating disorders, dissociation, feelings of helplessness and despair, anxiety, mood swings, and obsessive-compulsive thoughts. No wonder we feel like we're just one major event away from losing all sanity!

Understanding how trauma is stored in the body and that it needs to be released will help you for the rest of your life. You'll continually confront life experiences where you were forced to swallow down your true feelings and reactions. Those will be stored in your body, too.

Experiences like:
- a breakup or other major life change
- a major illness or injury
- the death of someone you love
- relationship issues, like cheating
- loss of a job, money, housing
- witnessing or being involved in violence
- discrimination, or racism

The effects of chronic fear and trauma as you're growing leaves lasting issues inside your brain and body. Add daily life experiences that leave you trembling with every big emotion known to man and you're in for a world of hurt if you don't heal.

If you've wondered why you can't remember anything, why your body aches all the time, why you're constantly running to the bathroom with an upset stomach, and just not operating at the same level as everyone else, then it sounds like you need to purge.

So congrats, babe. That's the first step is recognizing that you have trauma stored in your body in the first place.

The next step is to address and release it. Several therapeutic approaches can be effective in this process. (Hint: you will need to experiment with what works best for you).

This includes:

- **Somatic experiencing:** Somatic Experiencing is a healing method that focuses on how our bodies react to stress and works primarily with the nervous system. A therapist helps you notice and release tension in your body through simple exercises, like breathing deeply or moving in certain ways. This helps your body calm down and feel safe again, making it easier to heal from stress. Think of it as a way to bypass the brain and stay in the "here and now" to access more relaxation, containment, and emotional self-regulation.

- **Yoga and stretching:** Yoga and stretching can help release trauma from your body by relaxing muscles and calming your mind. When you're stressed or scared, your body can hold on to that tension, making you feel tight or uncomfortable. Yoga combines stretching, breathing, and gentle movements to help you notice and release this tension. The deep breathing and mindful movements in yoga can also help calm your nervous system, making you feel safer and more relaxed. This process helps your body let go of the stress and trauma it's been holding on to.

- **Mindfulness-based practices:** Mindfulness-based practices help release trauma by teaching you to focus on the present moment. When you're mindful, you pay attention to your thoughts, feelings, and body sensations without judging them. This helps you notice where your body is holding tension from past stress. By being aware and accepting these feelings, you can start to relax and let go of the tension. Mindfulness practices like meditation and deep breathing help calm your mind and body, making it easier to release the trauma and feel better.

- **Massage therapy:** Massage therapy for trauma release seeks to help the nervous system regulate itself to move out of the constant state of hyper-arousal and hyper-vigilance. Experiencing stress and tension can leave your muscles constricted and your body flooded with cortisol. Massage therapy has been shown to decrease cortisol levels while increasing hormones (serotonin and dopamine) associated with elevated mood. It also releases tension brought on by living in a state of fight or flight.

- **Cognitive processing therapy:** Cognitive Processing Therapy (CPT) helps release trauma by changing how you think about what happened. When you go through something really scary, it can leave you with upsetting thoughts and feelings. In CPT, a therapist helps you talk about the event and understand how it affects your thoughts and beliefs. They teach you to challenge and change negative thoughts, which can reduce stress and help your body relax. By thinking differently, you can feel less scared and more in control, helping your body release the trauma.

- **Eye movement desensitization and reprocessing:** Eye Movement Desensitization and Reprocessing (EMDR) helps release trauma and regulate your nervous system by using eye movements to process tough memories. When something really scary happens or if you're anxious something scary is going to happen, the memory can get stuck, causing stress. In EMDR, a therapist asks you to think about the event while following their finger with your eyes. This helps your brain reprocess the memory and emotions, making it less upsetting. As it becomes less intense, your nervous system calms down, reducing stress and helping your body feel more relaxed and in control.

- **Belly breathing:** Belly breathing (diaphragmatic breathing) may help release trauma from the body by reducing tension, lower your heart rate, blood pressure, and release deeply rooted pent-up energy in the subconscious.

- **Shaking:** Shaking or vibrating helps you burn through excess adrenaline and release tension in your muscles. It's a fast way to calm the nervous system and allow it to get back to its neutral state. Shaking activates a natural reflex mechanism in your body that signals the danger has passed. You can turn off flight-or-fight, and the nervous system can return to normal.

- **Emotional Freedom Technique (EFT) Tapping:** Emotional Freedom Technique (EFT) Tapping involves tapping on specific points of the body to help manage emotions and troubling thoughts. It's unique in that it combines traditional Chinese medicine with modern psychological acupressure techniques and components of cognitive behavioral therapies and exposure therapy.

These methods focus on restoring the body-mind connection, releasing stored tension, and promoting self-regulation. Go through exercises with a counselor or psychologist. If you can't afford that, then read books like *Happy Days: The Guided Path from Trauma to Profound Freedom and Inner Peace* by Gabrielle Bernstein. Or *The Mountain Is You: Transforming Self-Sabotage Into Self-Mastery* by Brianna Wiest. Even watching YouTube videos and following along is better than doing nothing. I've learned a lot from YouTube. There's no shame in that!

This isn't a one-time fix. You won't be cured after trying one of the methods above one time. These are techniques that require ongoing commitment. But that's ok, because you're worth the time it takes to get your body and mind to a good place! I've used many of the tactics above and still have a few I use a couple times a week. Something as simple as retreating to the bathroom and shaking out my arms can help reset my nervous system so I can continue with my day instead of getting sidelined with anxiety.

Design Your "Panic Post-it"

Creating a "Panic Post-it" is a simple yet powerful tool to help you navigate those tough moments. I also really like this idea because I can remove the post-its when company comes over, so no one knows I have reminders in my kitchen to help me not lose my shit (well, ok, now everyone knows because of this book, but that's ok.)

By keeping this little note in key spots like your kitchen or bathroom (or anywhere else, you'll have quick reminders of stress-relief techniques right in front of you when you need them most. Here's how to create your own Panic Post-it:

Step 1: Choose Your Spot

Decide where you'll place your Panic Post-it. The goal is to have it in a location where you'll see it frequently, so consider sticking it:

- On your fridge or a kitchen cabinet door.
- On the bathroom mirror or next to the shower.
- Or, why not both? The more reminders, the better!

Step 2: Pick Your Techniques

Think about the stress-relief activities that resonate with you. What helps you feel calmer or more centered? Choose activities you can do on your own right away (verses waiting to see your therapist). Here are some options you might include on your post-it:

- Emotional Freedom Technique (EFT) Tapping
- Yoga and Stretching
- Mindfulness-Based Practices
- Eye Movement Desensitization and Reprocessing (EMDR)
- Belly Breathing
- Shaking or Vibrating

Step 3: Write It Down

On your post-it, write down specific actions you're going to take from the techniques that you find most helpful. Keep it simple and clear—this is your quick-reference guide during moments of stress. For example, your Panic Post-it might look something like this:

- 10 deep belly breaths.
- Tap and repeat "I'm anxious but I'm safe."
- Lumbar twist stretch.
- Wash hands with cold water.

Step 4: Stick It Up

Once you've written your reminders, place the post-it where you'll see it often. The kitchen and bathroom are perfect spots because they're places you visit multiple times a day.

Step 5: Use It Regularly

Whenever you're feeling stressed, take a moment to refer to your Panic Post-it. Let it guide you through the techniques that help you feel more grounded and in control. Over time, these practices can become second nature, helping you navigate the healing process with greater ease.

Bonus, your family or roommates might find this beneficial, too!

You are an *incredible* being, and hopefully your panic post-it will help you remember that! Download the worksheet "Activities to Release Fear and Damage From Trauma" at VillainEraGoddess.com for links to YouTube videos with explanations and examples of the healing practices above, as well as links to meditations and recommended books.

👑 *I give you permission to research the hell out of how the body stores trauma. Start moving your body in meaningful ways and reach out for help. This is important and vital to your happiness and coming out of your villain era feeling like a true goddess.*

I FEEL GOOD.

9. ACTING NORMAL WHILE HEALING

Accept your inner crazy bitch.

Listen. If someone's going to be saying outrageous shit, it's going to be me.

I see jokes all the time about how as women age we stop giving a fuck, and start saying the most offensive shit. And dammit if that doesn't sound like a good time to me.

Because I've changed. Somewhere along this trek of forging my own trail, fighting monsters, putting band aids on blisters because it turns out this was an uphill hike, I forgot how to wear my fake face. My villainous journey seemed to have wiped all faux pleasantry from my personality and replaced it with whatever the hell I'm feeling at the moment.

If you spend most of your life trying to make yourself smaller and more socially acceptable, then get ready. Once the lid blows off, you can't shove yourself back down, and it's a wild ride for quite some time.

"The Keepers of the Status Quo" want you to mask anger, disagreement, and other strong emotions that make *them* uncomfortable. "They" are made of anyone who benefits from keeping you small and quiet so they can continue using you.

This goes beyond the "hey why don't you smile more" vermin who litter sidewalks. It also includes the quiet old lady who says, "I'd never talk to my husband like that!" The guy who doesn't move out of the way on the sidewalk because he already knows you'll be the first to move. The teacher in college who paired you with the loud boy who never completes his work so you could do the work for two. The grocery store manager who calls you darling and touches your arm too much. The barf-bag of a man who keeps trying to keep eye contact for too long, like you two are sharing a damn moment instead of just standing in line to pay for your pads and tampons.

If you tried to call any of those people out, you'd be met with shocked, upset reactions. They're just trying to help. They're just trying to be nice. They didn't think you'd mind because you're always so nice. I'm sure you've heard it all!

So, what happens when you stop making them comfortable? Well, at first you're all uncomfortable, *even you*. Surprise! This is new territory for all of you and you might feel discomfort in this area, too.

Where Did the Social Anxiety Come From?

In my twenties, even in my early thirties, I would have been *horrified* to think that someone thought I was unpleasant. After all, I was always "such a treat" as the well-meaning but definitely status-quo-keeping older ladies would tell my mother.

But then I changed. I morphed into one of those "*I don't think so*" and "*What did you mean by that?*" women who look you in the eye for three seconds longer than is socially acceptable and judge you based on her rules. These women are unpredictable. A woman who *actually responds* instead of just looking pleasant is scary. I joined these female warriors and stopped masking my feelings for offensive people and situations.

Once I stopped, I had to deal with the disappointment and reactions of those who were counting on me being *pleasant*, but instead got *honest*. This is when my anxiety really started to come out to play. It turns out I had been maneuvering through landmines with a smile on my face for years, and I was exhausted. I was resentful, and I was pissed, and I was in a brand new territory—this territory was the opposite of people pleasing.

Conversations changed as I stopped giving these people the easy way out of a tough conversation. I stopped laughing off their dumb jokes and started letting my face show what I wanted it to say. I was proud of myself for being authentic. But something else came with it…
a huge barge floating down the river, full of social anxiety. I wasn't used to being the disagreeable person in the room and I wasn't used to seeing people view *me* as offensive. My anxiety was overwhelming by the time I got home from social settings. I'd sit in my room and think through everything I said, every look or glance I received from anyone.

This unlocked a whole new level of exhaustion for me, because not only was I having anxiety about the tough conversations, I was also starting to have anxiety about the *good* conversations, too. Was I too much? Have I changed too much? All the questions all the time on a loop in my head, and it made me want to just stay home and hide from everyone, even friends.

I knew I had to find a way to honor my own feelings, not be fake, and feel good about it. And I had to stop smothering myself with anxiety when I got home. I didn't want to go back to being fake, but holy shit, this new level of anxiety was killing me. I felt like I was on full display all the time.

The good news was that I had spent so much time giving myself self-love and healing that I forgot how to tone myself down. I forgot how to sit quietly and nod.

The bad news was that I didn't know what to do with my "new" self.

Where is the Anger Coming From?

Part of my "new" self was honoring the anger inside my body. A certain level of anger comes with having your eyes opened to the bullshit around you. For me, it started slow. I set a boundary and told my story, and then three things happened.

1. Family members started opening up about their own stories, and I was able to put a bigger picture together of the abuse that happened in our family. Seeing the bigger picture of how manipulated and controlled we were by gaslighters and abusers was infuriating!

2. Other family members said I was making things up and that I've "changed." I was no longer my sweet self, and I seemed angry and mean now. This was one of their final arguments after losing control over my voice and body. These judgements from abusers about *my* actions as I started standing up for myself brought about a level of rage I wasn't prepared for.

3. Another group, the people who don't see the patterns, who haven't done the work I've done—thought I was suddenly mean and angry *from out of nowhere*. I call these people the "floaters"—they're floating through life in their own world and aren't necessarily inclined to try to see things from your point of view. They don't want to deal with your messiness. It's not that they don't believe you, they just don't want to be involved. They "just want everyone to get along." The actions of these people inadvertently keep the gas lighters and abusers lifted up, protecting them whether they mean to or not.

All of these scenarios left me angry. And that's the rub. You *will* be angry. I mean, how could we not be angry? I was livid that I found myself in the role of the "villain"... while the actual villains sat protected.

My anger scared me at first. I grew up thinking that anger was something to be avoided at all costs. "Don't say or do something out of anger" was a phrase I heard over and over. So, how was I supposed to navigate my villain era while I had anger rising in me? I grew up fearing angry people, and I didn't want to be one of those people.

This was another new aspect of myself that I didn't know what to do with.

Where are the Blow Ups Coming From?

Remember when you were a kid and you fell off your bike, your mom had to help you roll your pant leg up past your knees so she could see the wound? Unfortunately, your pants are stuck to your wound, it hurts like hell, and now your wound is exposed to the air and is stinging even more. Your first instinct is to yell "OUCH!"

That's what starting your villain era is like. The healing process starts by exposing those wounds, and now they are super sensitive. You want to protect it at all costs. But then there comes some asshole who is used to pulling shenanigans with no consequences, and you're going to yell whatever the equivalent of OUCH is for that moment.

The gaslighters have been waiting for this. As soon as you yell OUCH they swoop in to tell you how rude you are, how inappropriate and unnecessary your actions were—things you were already thinking about yourself. The gaslighters love policing how we stick up for ourselves and love pointing out if you yell OUCH too loudly.

Now here come the dark, heavy clouds of anxiety and anger, too. Making this a bundle of newness that doesn't seem much better than the old you.

Normal vs. New

When your "normal" is taken away, it's going to cause you some inner turmoil. Even if "normal" was wrong for you, it was still *your* normal.

It's as if you've had your head down, creating a brand new path for yourself, and when you look up, the scenery around you isn't of a forest or an ocean or anything recognizable. It's a kaleidoscope of disorienting colors. Everything is changing. You are changing, how you process thoughts is changing, how much you put up with from others is changing, how you bond with others is changing. It's an unfamiliar setting you find yourself in.

You may feel like you're suddenly unsure of how to behave in every social situation. You know you have boundaries—you don't want to be a doormat. Plus, you want to soak up all the fun times with friends, but then what? How?

The Other Shoe. Where Is It?

This part of your healing journey—the part that sets you up to be an unstoppable villainous queen—is all about innerwork. You need to stop pre-judging yourself before entering a social setting and post-judging yourself after leaving a social setting.

Be careful that after you've released the hold other peoples' judgments have over you, that you don't subconsciously step in to fill that role for them. Those judgments were part of your old normal, not your amazing new normal.

Stop judging yourself and waiting for the other shoe to drop. It's normal to feel a bit freaked out when your normal is replaced with new and you're still adjusting. Be patient while you get settled in with your new boundaries and reactions.

Breathe and Journal Through Social Anxiety

If anxiety is hitting you hard during this stage, then you need to journal. This is a wonderful way to release pent-up emotions but also to take a deep dive into your feelings and emotions and decide if they're true or false (because guess what—your brain is all about lying to you and making shit up).

When you get home, anxiety can tell you all kinds of lies: everyone hates you, your jokes were annoying, you didn't handle the tough conversations well, you were barely tolerated by your friends and family... whatever else your lovely mind brings up for you. When this happens, recognize this as your mind trying to set you back to normal mode and you have to fight it. Your greatest weapon is pen and paper.

Journal about your situation:
- What situation are you feeling anxious about?
- What do you think you did wrong?
- What do you wish you would have done differently?
- And now... do you think that would have made a difference? Do you think you're just being hard on yourself?
- Do you think these extreme thoughts are hurting you?
- What would you tell your BFF who was having these thoughts?
- What were some of the good parts of this social interaction?
- What are some kind words you can tell yourself?

When you're done, take five deep breaths and say out loud, "Let it go." Yes, I know, this ain't *Frozen* and you ain't Elsa, but it does work!

Honor Anger

Listen, I'm not asking you to throw yourself on the floor screaming. Or yell nasty things to the people who hurt you—although I fantasize about that often. But tucking your anger deep inside of you and hiding it isn't healthy either.

First of all, anger is normal. Especially when you're healing, setting boundaries, reinforcing boundaries, reinforcing boundaries *again*, and dealing with abusers and gaslighters who are spewing whatever they can to keep the status quo.

And second, anger should be honored. It's the huge rotating light at the top of a lighthouse that can help guide you if you let it. Sudden anger could be letting you know that someone or something just triggered you or you're not being respected.

Sitting with your anger and studying it can help you get a better look at what's going on. I have a family member who is super pleasant while things are going her way, but is condescending and passive aggressive when she wants to manipulate me into making a decision that she thinks is better for me. She's super subtle about it.

Well, it felt subtle until I stopped swallowing down my anger and instead studied it. I'd get home and think through my conversation with her because I couldn't figure out where my very sudden burst of anger came from while we were talking. It took me a bit to see the pattern and I would have just kept getting triggered if I wouldn't have started studying my anger.

Now when I'm chatting with her and I get a sudden surge of red hot anger flooding my body, I can quickly assess the words that just came out of her mouth and realize that she's trying to manipulate me and my subconscious caught her in the act. I can now adjust the conversation, set my boundary, and move on.

Honoring anger means it can move through you instead of getting stuck in your body and causing sickness. It means you can learn from it instead of hiding from it.

I do agree that if you're angry, you should not yell out personal insults that you might regret later. But that doesn't mean you need to keep your mouth shut. You can yell out the truth. You can scream your boundaries out loud. I think that's ok. You'll eventually settle down and stop screaming.

The longer I sat with my anger, the more gratitude I felt for it. I felt the rage for my inner child. I felt rage as a mom. I felt rage as a sister. I let the rage heal me. I was enraged on my own behalf and I still won't let anyone take that feeling away from me. It doesn't run my life. But I honor it because I need someone to feel it on my behalf and that person will be me.

Journaling is great for anger, too! Ask yourself:
- Where is this coming from?
- What happened right before I felt angry?
- What emotions sit under this anger?

Next, give yourself a pep talk—or end your journal entry with one—and tell yourself that it's ok to feel anger. Take deep breaths, shake your arms to release the energy, and know that you're a force to be reckoned with.

Give Yourself Grace *Publicly*

Good grief, we give everyone around us so many allowances while holding ourselves to a higher standard. It's time to stop expecting perfection and love yourself how you are right now today.

Did you yell at an abuser or gaslighter today? Did you scream OUCH or its equivalent when they hurt you today? That's ok. It's ok. You're ok. You're amazing at standing up for yourself.

Give yourself grace and *let it be known* that you give yourself permission to be who you need to be. One of the biggest fears I see from other women during this stage is how to respond to the gaslighters and abusers when they go into attack mode. This is how you respond:

- When someone says you're acting crazy? You say: *Yeah, I like it better this way.*

- When someone says you suddenly have a nasty attitude? You say: *Well, aren't you lucky to see this rare side of me.*

- When someone says you're not acting very Christian-like? You say: *You're not a gatekeeper of Christ and I'll get his opinions on my own.*

- When someone says that you're upsetting the family? You say: *My family is doing just fine. I don't know who you're referring to.*

- When someone says they are disappointed in your behavior? You say: *I can no longer hold space in my life for your feelings. You'll need to deal with that disappointment on your own.*

- When someone says you're going to regret acting this way? You say: *I already don't regret it.*

We're so used to these fuckers lording over us, it's easy to go into freeze or fawn mode when the attacks start. Give yourself grace to stick up for yourself in the most imperfect, messy ways.

And hey, if it gets to be too much, just say you're having raging diarrhea and leave or hang up the phone. (In my experience, diarrhea is always an excellent excuse to leave a situation.)

Navigating This New World

When you first start navigating this new world, it's a bit like holding a new map full of roads and locations you've never heard of before. You have to orient yourself while flying down the freeway at eighty miles an hour knowing you have an exit coming up, but you're not sure which one.

As you move through this period of your life for a bit longer, you'll become more familiar with your new world and will start to enjoy your surroundings.

I give you permission to accept the mess that you are during this process. Yes, be gentle with yourself while popping the bubbles of anxiety until they dissipate into nothing. But also, hone your anger as a tool of self-guidance, like a blacksmith creating a sword. And when you lay your sword down for the day, give yourself all the grace in the world so it feels like you're returning to a comfy bed full of soft blankets that smell like lavender and ylang ylang. You are your safe place, and it's ok to act like it.

I'D RATHER BE WHERE I AM RIGHT NOW THAN WHERE I WAS LAST YEAR.

10. LOSING FRIENDS WHILE FINDING YOURSELF

Embracing change and letting go of blame.

First of all, I'm delightful.

During the beginning of your villain era, you'll find that you will lose yourself.

You'll lose how you view yourself. What your main priorities are. How you navigate life. It's all turned upside down, hidden, lost, and up to you to find.

Through soul searching, shadow work, therapy, and perseverance, you'll eventually find yourself again. Then after you find yourself, well… you start to lose friends. This part of the journey can feel like a mindfuck full of ups and downs that doesn't allow you to relax or let your guard down.

While your metamorphosis is happening on the inside, it's affecting every single area of your life on the outside. The pilgrimage to villainhood can be filled with big emotions and ass-loads of insecurity, which can make you more sensitive to losing friends.

You know you're working on yourself to change for the better and you're getting stronger, setting boundaries, and starting to feel proud of yourself… but then you start losing friends. This can lead to second guessing yourself. Maybe you're too much. Maybe you shouldn't talk about your journey with them. Maybe you should go back to being your old self. It takes a lot of self-reflection and self-*support* to get through this.

I think we're more emotional during this part of the journey because we're realizing how broken we are and we're asking others to love us not only for who we are but also for who we want to be. We're asking others to agree that we're making the right decision to start cutting out toxic, abusive people. We're asking them to support us while we build the confidence needed to get more assertive about how others treat us. Any rejection cuts so deep it feels like your bone marrow is exposed to freezing cold air.

That's how it was for me. I cut toxic, unsafe family out of my life during the peak of my villain era. Even though they weren't good people, I still felt the empty, physical space left in my life. However, I also *knew without a doubt* that I would automatically fill that empty space with love from my friends. When some friends didn't want to fill that space, it hurt. Being ghosted or phased out of a friendship is a blow to your confidence and makes you more self-conscious when it comes to navigating pretty much every other relationship in your life.

A few years ago, I set an intention to strengthen my circle of friends. I was feeling stuck in life and kept seeing the same message over and over— even though I wasn't looking for it.

While listening to podcasts, reading email, reading books, and watching YouTube videos, the exact same message kept popping up. "You're the average of the five people you spend the most time with." This is part of a larger quote from motivational speaker Jim Rohn, that also includes, "Show me your friends and I'll show you your future." I know there are mixed feelings about this quote, but it really spoke to me. Just like a person who can't hang out with alcoholics when they're giving up alcohol, a villain era goddess needs to reevaluate who she's hanging out with, too.

This was a glaring spotlight directly into my eyeballs. I had been trying to change how I showed up in life and how I talked about my life and the future. I wanted to be more positive. I wanted to set boundaries *with myself* on the types of conversations I had in my leisure time with friends and with how I wanted to behave. I wanted my everyday conversations to include statements to the universe that would build the life I wanted.

So I sat in my backyard under the full moon and set an intention to release habits and, if needed, friendships that were affecting how I showed up for myself, for my family, for my dreams. If something was holding me back from being the best person I could be, then I needed to let it (or them) go.

Well, I got what I asked for. Within a month, a close friend completely ghosted me. She didn't know I set this intention (no one did). And I did think about her a little bit when I set it. She was negative about money, family, and work—even during fun events. However, all of that said, I had a lot of fun with her and enjoyed her friendship. I had been interested to see where our friendship went next after setting my full moon intention. Turns out, it went into a pile of burning sewage. She ghosted me that summer and my heart still aches from it. Even though I literally asked for this, it still hurt.

The insecurity that bloomed inside of me from being ghosted stayed in my body for a while and honestly, still pops up from time to time. I knew I wasn't pure trash. I still had friends, but it *hurt*. I also knew it was up to me to get over this on my own with love and kindness so I could continue toward my goal of positivity.

To do that, I needed to reframe how I thought about lost friendships so I could move on. I started reading more about friendships and relationships and why we choose people and reject people. I've walked away with an understanding that we're all just doing what we have to do to survive and that evolves over time. Unfortunately, not all friendships last because we're constantly changing. I needed to accept this on a higher level so I could apply it to an individual level.

Understanding Different Realities

To understand this on a higher level, I had to understand that we're all constantly changing and no one is living the exact same experience.

How you perceive the world and perceive yourself affects how *you* see others and how *you* react to the world around you.

On the flip side, how others react toward you is based on how *they* perceive the world and how *they* perceive you as they watch you react to the world around you.

No one is the same. Each of your friends sees you as a completely different person. I see my best friend in a wholly different way than others do.

Which person's reality is correct? Which is the most accurate? Put everyone in a big room together and you all will walk out with people ranked from your most favorite to least favorite and it's different for everyone.

I think the answer is that everyone is correct.

And this is why friendships and relationships are so weird. Our realities, and perceptions based on those realities, are constantly shifting. Someone you fell madly in love with one year ago repulses you now. Your reality shifted and now you're not a match. This goes for friendships, too. Your realities shift, causing you to drift in different directions or maybe even collide.

Everyone reading this is thinking of someone they grew apart from. Someone they just stopped talking to as often, didn't invite over anymore, slowly pulled away from. And you have your reasoning for why you pulled away. It makes perfect sense to you.

The problem? It stops making sense when *you're* the person who is left out. When others stop calling *you*, stop inviting *you* over. Once you're the victim of shifting realities and perceptions, this theory doesn't feel so comfortable anymore.

Suddenly, this whole thing feels rigged.

The shifts, the waves, they're happening all the time. We're all changing for the better or for the worse. We're moving forward on our own journeys.

This is why friendships are so fucking hard—they can end. And when you feel like it was at your expense, it hits you right in the gut. And now you have to give someone grace who hurt your feelings. You have to look at the bigger picture and understand that their reality and perceptions shifted, too, and they don't feel they are a fit for you. Allowing that movement, that shift, out of your life without drama is a test of how far you are on your journey.

Trust the Process

Gawd, that sounds lame. "Trust the process" . . . but it's true.

When you start growing more confident and making big moves to protect yourself and your family, including setting boundaries, and most importantly, talking about it, you're going to lose friends. Your trauma makes you a perfect fit for some friends. When you heal that trauma, you're not a fit anymore.

But, it's not just friends leaving you—you'll be leaving friends behind, too. You'll be the bad guy in *their* reality. I've found this out the hard way. That's why it's important to give grace.

Even though this process hurts, it's not your fault. And truthfully, it's probably not really their fault either. Walking away from this without hating the other person is a lesson in growth. You can choose to let them go and let the hurt go.

I'm in a better place now. I still miss that friend, but I'm now surrounded by people who have less jealousy, who complain less about their families, who look forward to the future more, who align more with who I want to be and how I want to show up. Friends who text or Snap me at least once a day. Friends who invite me to do fun things based on my likes and wants, not just theirs. Friends who are so amazing, I feel like I can never show enough of my gratitude for them.

Find Your "Rowers"

This chapter isn't about feeling sad for what we lost (we put our tap shoes away, remember?!), this is about learning how to rebuild your foundation of support in a way that leaves you excited with glitter falling from the sky and a pep in your step.

Life really is just all of us trying to successfully navigate rocky waters. As soon as the first wave hits, some people will jump off the boat while grabbing the very last life preserver. But others will surprise you by grabbing an oar and rowing with you. *Celebrate the rowers.*

There are two steps you can take to find your rowers and let go of any hurt from those jumping ship.

1. Review your list of your friends. This sounds like something you might do during middle-school while being stuck in a gymnasium on a raining day, but you need to start here. Take an honest look at your friendships. Who lifts you up? Who puts as much energy toward you as you do to them? Use the "Build a friend" checklist to honestly review your friendships.
2. Start letting go. However a friendship ended (ghosting, breakup, phased out), you need to cut ties with any emotional pain you're still holding on to. You can do this through the chord cutting ceremony outlined later in this chapter.

Creating Your Own Tight Circle of Support

Friendships are influenced by the ebb and flow of life's circumstances and understanding this can help ease the sting of friendships that come to a close.

Career changes, family commitments, long distances, and personal challenges will change you and can impact the energy you invest in maintaining relationships.

If you're feeling like your friends list needs a bit of tweaking, start by categorizing the kinds of friends you want. It's not fair to ask one person to be everything to you!

This step is important because it helps you understand that you may need to lighten up on your friends, too. And some of your friends might not need to be held to the same standards as others.

Your categories might look different, but here are mine:

- Accomplishing goals and accountability
- Business or work network
- Fitness
- Hobbies
- Friends with kids who are the same age
- Vacation/weekend trip friends
- The super close friends who will help me bury a body

Not all of these friends are interested in or can offer the support you need in all of these areas. Some of my best friends to travel with and have fun with couldn't care less about my business and goals. They don't get it and wouldn't say the right thing even if I asked for advice. And that's fine! It's not their job to be ALL THAT I NEED. It's my job to find and create my circles to meet my needs.

The "Build a Friend" Checklist

Next, it's important to ensure you're surrounding yourself with people who align with your values, support your growth, and bring out the best in you (and that you bring out the best in them as well!). It's always good to review these questions at least once a year when evaluating how you show up in the world and how your friends impact that.

- What are my core values?
- Am I willing to invest time and effort?
- What are my boundaries?
- How do my friends and I communicate and handle conflict?
- Do they inspire personal growth?
- How do they treat others?
- Do we share similar values of trust and loyalty?
- Do I feel comfortable being myself around them?

Next, make sure the friendship isn't one-sided. Being the only one running the circus can suck up too much of your energy and mental health. Check in honestly with yourself.

- Who initiates convos (even just sending you memes) with you?
- Who blows you off?
- What are your friends' strengths and weaknesses?
- How do your friends try to connect with you?

Don't forget to take a hard look at yourself as well.

- What are your good traits?
- Are you a good friend? Calling/texting/asking them to hang out?
- What do friends like about you? (You can ask them if you want!)

- How do you try to connect with your friends?

Use these answers to help evaluate your current friends and then to help you look at what's missing. The wonderfully unexpected outcome of this exercise is that it can help you to step back and see where you're not being a great friend, either. I realized I had some friends texting me every day, and I was so focused on someone ghosting me that I didn't take the time to appreciate the ones who love me deeply.

And lastly, if you were ghosted, phased out, or friend-dumped, please take a quiet moment to surround yourself in love and just focus on healing. If you were hanging out with your ten-year-old self, what would you say to her if she lost a friend? Tell yourself those kind, supportive words.

Cord Cutting Ceremony

Friendships are dynamic relationships which evolve and morph over time. As we grow and change, it's essential to understand that these transformations are not personal failures or shortcomings. That said, it still hurts when they don't work out. I like to use cord cutting ceremonies when I'm letting go of a friendship or when I want to let go of an old narrative in a current friendship so I can allow that relationship to regrow in a healthy way that works for both of us.

What Are Cords And Why Do We Need to Cut Them?

Energetic cords are non-physical connections formed between individuals, things, or places through emotions, relationships, or experiences. These cords are not visible to the naked eye but exist on an energetic level, influencing the way we feel and interact with others. While some cords are positive and nourishing, others may be draining or detrimental to our emotional and mental health. For instance, a cord with a toxic relationship may keep us trapped in negative patterns, plunge us into depression and anxiety, and prevent personal growth and healing. An Energetic Cord Cutting Ceremony is a ritual that involves severing those energetic ties that bind us to people, allowing us to reclaim our energy and power. Cutting a cord with a toxic person will give you much needed relief from the drama that surrounds them.

By consciously severing these cords, you'll create an opportunity for personal liberation, increased self-awareness, overall relief, and the restoration of your energy. This process helps you reclaim your power and establish healthy boundaries. This is a favorite ritual of mine and has helped me so many times to get out of my head and stop worrying about the other person.

Give yourself ten minutes of uninterrupted time to complete your own cord cutting ceremony with the following instructions.

<u>You will need:</u>
- Incense, sage stick, palo santo stick, or other dried herbs
- Lighter
- Small rock of your choice
- Optional: white candle and a pen or pencil to carve words into the candle

<u>Clear Your Space</u>

Purify the energy around you and any items you're using during this ritual, including yourself, with smoke from dried herbs (like a sage or palo santo stick) or incense. During this step, you're basically ensuring the energy is like a blank slate with no intent or outside influence and setting up a barrier from anything negative. As you move the smoke around your space and items, stay in the moment and focus on the intent of cleansing your space. You can chant a mantra to stay focused if you'd like. "I replace any negative energy in this space with the highest and best energy." Picture a sparkly bubble around you that allows only good, truthful things in and blocks everything else out.

Set Your Intention

This part is optional and you don't need it in order to have a successful cord cutting ceremony, but I also like to light a candle to double down on my intentions. Write "peace" or "release" on the candle before lighting it. Tea candles are a great option here because they are small and you can let them burn out naturally after a ritual.

Identify Energetic Cord Connections

Next, it's time to identify the cords you wish to release and clarify your desire for personal growth and healing. I prefer to do this while standing because it's easier to visualize my entire body.

Set your candle on the floor in front of you if you are able to set it down in a safe spot. Next, set your rock down next to the candle. You can use a gemstone or just a rock from your backyard. It's your conduit, but there aren't any official rules around which rock to use.

Next, close your eyes. Thank the rock for aiding you in the ritual and then ask it to show you the cords you have connecting you with a particular person. You can say, "Show me the energetic cords I have with [insert person's name]."

Whatever comes to your mind, just let it come, don't overthink it. Your rock will show you where the energetic cords attach to your body. There could be multiple cords in different areas of your body and they can have different thicknesses.

Cut Energetic Cords

Once your rock shows you the cords, use your hand like a sword and slice the cord off your body where it attaches to you. While removing the cord, say, "I release my ties with [person's name], allowing us both to find peace. Harm no one." Say this each time you cut a cord off your body. This ensures you're doing this ritual with the intent for both of you to have peace.

Celebrate the Healthy Cords

This part is fun! When you're finished with the cord cutting, before wrapping things up, ask your rock to show you the cords you have with someone you absolutely adore. This will show you what a good, positive, healthy cord looks like. Check them out! Look at how gorgeous and strong they are! Look at how you're connected to those you love! Take a moment to appreciate what you have.

When you are finished, thank your rock and put it back where you found it or in a special location if you're going to keep it for these purposes in the future. Thank the fire in the candle and either let it finish burning or blow it out.

You're done! How do you feel?

👑 *You have my permission to give a high-five and a hearty goodbye to those who jumped ship during your villain era journey. And then move on to create welcome baskets full of lotions, THC-infused candy bars, and cucumber eye masks for those who came aboard with an oar, sunscreen, and a funny story that leaves you giggling while the salty sea air blows through your hair. We're focusing on the good and moving forward with positivity and the wonderful people who support us!*

I'M SO GRATEFUL FOR MY WONDERFUL GROUP OF FRIENDS.

11. BUILDING SELF WORTH AND CONFIDENCE

Focus on self-love.

Asking for a friend: Which came first? Self-worth or confidence?

Confidence is such a tricky bitch, am I right?

If you were beaten down emotionally, mentally, or physically as a kid, you might not have much self-worth sparkling along the insides of your body. You probably hesitate when it's time to say something kind about yourself. You probably shrug away years' worth of experience at work and let others take the lead because you're not sure if you're qualified. You probably don't make eye contact with the cute person across the room because you already know they can find someone better.

I'm a high performer at work, I am a great mom, I'm a good partner, but I'd never felt confident. And I felt like a failure every single time confidence didn't drape across my shoulders like armor. The words self-love, self-worth, and self-confidence were such elusive terms and had always felt out of reach. I used to think ascending to the euphoric stage of my life where self-confidence pulsed off my body in waves meant that I'd made it. I imagined Confident Ashley walking down the street in four-inch heels looking like a runway model, the wind blowing her hair behind her as people gasp in wonder as their gaze falls upon her. Like a unicorn! But without a horn, or the body of a horse, and in heels. Well, you get it.

Turns out that's not what it feels like to have confidence. It also turns out that self-worth doesn't feel like that either. And, come to find out, confidence and self-worth have nothing to do with each other and you don't need one for the other. The only thing they have in common is that self-love is the answer to achieving both.

Here me out, I'll explain.

Building Yourself up with Self Love

I didn't realize how far I'd come in my journey of self-love until I was helping my mom go through dusty, beat-up boxes full of memories after my dad passed away. She found old photos of our family on different vacations throughout the years.

As I was looking through the photos, I came to a photo of ten-year-old me and the other four kids of our blended family. We were huddled together on the back of a boat floating down the dirty water of the Mississippi River. We had our arms wrapped around each other, smiling big and standing as close as we could while wearing huge, bright orange life jackets. Our skin was kissed by glowing rays of sunshine and we were so happy. I looked at that photo and zeroed in on myself, thinking, "Oh my gosh, I was *such* a cute kid."

Then I sat back, shocked as shit, because I realized I'd never once in my life looked at a photo of myself and thought "cute" or looked at myself and was content with what I'd seen. In the past, when looking at photos of a younger Ashley, I'd think, "Wow, I'm so glad people were still my friends even though I looked like this." Or "I'm so grateful people felt sorry enough for me to be my friend." Like I was a hideous troll with tusks, a beard, and a pronounced overbite. Instead of a skinny, long-legged goofy kid who laughed at all the fart jokes and just wanted to pet all the animals.

I grew up with an older sister who had gone through horrible abuse at the hands of trusted family members. We both suffered, but she was most often victimized and often put herself in harm's way to protect me.

These abusers ruined so much of our childhood and turned my sister into a shell of self-loathing, and many times, her hurt was turned toward me. I suffered a lot of abuse from her, but her most consistent approach to dishing out hurt was to take me aside each day to remind me that I was ugly, I was fat, I was stupid, and no one liked me. That anyone who was nice to me was only doing so because they felt bad for me.

If she was having a particularly bad day, she'd dig her long, sharp fingernails into my hands and arms until I bled as she recited these daily reminders to me. As we grew older, her abuse happened in different ways, but the message was always the same. Looking back, I can see that she was projecting onto me what she felt about herself, but the damage was done. I saw myself as hideous. When I left home, I stepped in to fill the role of telling myself that I was ugly, fat, and stupid each day since my sister wasn't there to do it for me.

That chilly Saturday on the family farm, I held that photo in my hands and . . . well, honestly, I told myself sternly, "Don't you dare fucking cry until you get home."

So, I held it in and then bawled the whole way home. The realization that I *loved* me shocked me to my core. I'd fist fight anyone who said I wasn't a cute kid. I was a little blessing and a ray of sunshine. I loved ten-year-old Ashley with her long, tangled hair pulled back with a big barrette on the side of her head (it was the 90s), with her big smile, eyes squinting in the sun, nose crinkled from smiling and squinting, looking like she knew an inside joke, and knobby knees bracing herself as the boat rocked in the waves.

She was *fucking adorable*, and I wanted her to know that when I saw her smiling face, I was grinning right back at her like a proud mama. I'd been hugging her metaphorically for a while now as I healed. But to come face to face with her through this photo brought me to tears.

I had been practicing self-love every day. Loving my inner child, giving my mean inner voice grace as I told it I disagreed with it, and doing shadow work to heal myself. Having this moment, looking at this photo, where I see all my hard work pay off was the reward I needed. And let me tell you, I BAWLED. Tears, snot, swollen eyes bawled. It was wonderful.

Showing my inner child unconditional love was slowly building my self-worth piece by piece. Pulling pieces of myself back to my body, claiming those pieces in whatever shape I found them in—even if they were broken and decayed and didn't fit perfectly. I was showing them love, telling them it wasn't their fault while wiping the shame off them.

Cutting off the decay to make way for new growth and using kindness to fill in the missing gaps around the pieces that didn't quite fit yet. They're my pieces and I will continue doing the hard work of holding this broken body together with love until it can stand up on its own. Because I'm worth the work it takes, and I love providing that effort to myself.

Self-Love Over Confidence Every Time

You know what I didn't need to do all of this? Self-confidence.

And thankfully, I didn't wait around for self-confidence to appear out of thin air like the Ghost of Christmas Past or I'd still be waiting. When I said confidence was a tricky bitch, what I really meant to say was that confidence is a little fucking bitch-ass trickster and I want to fight her.

If you're entering your villain era and you're waiting for confidence before you stand up to family, friends, co-workers, or whoever you need to set boundaries with, then you might be disappointed when you find yourself all alone with no confidence at your back, ready to step up and make you feel like you have the strength of a warrior.

Here's what I've learned. Confidence comes *after* you do the thing. Whatever the thing is. It never comes to you *before* you do it when you're sitting at home wishing you had it. Confidence is earned through *doing*, not achieved through wishing. Honestly, not even achieved through affirmations. See why I call confidence so many nasty things? Like, thanks for nothing, ya bitch.

When it's time to stand up for yourself and your hands are shaking, your throat is tight, and you can feel the tears sitting behind your eyes hot and ready to spill down your cheeks, it can feel so overwhelming and daunting. Like instead of sticking up for yourself, you should just hide under the closest thing that has at least five inches of clearance space.

Here Comes Self Worth

This is when self-worth comes into play. Instead of focusing on gathering confidence, focus on fostering self-worth. And then step forward and say what you need to say.

People who tout confidence will say that with confidence you'll be able to better communicate your boundaries and messages to the people you're standing up to (I'm talking about *you*, Instagram influencers, with your glossy hair and dagger nails acting like you have it figured out). Fuck that. Thinking that way will only make you feel like a failure before you begin.

You gotta stand up while still shaking, babe. You gotta speak while you're crying, with snot running onto your lip. You scream if you have to, you look ugly if you have to, but you get it done. And when you're all finished and shaking in your car, driving home or retreating to your bedroom crying, you'll hear something *magnificent*. A sweet little voice inside of you quietly saying, "Thank you."

What you didn't realize is that you just practiced self-love. By standing up for yourself, you provided protection and love that you didn't receive as a kid. And giving yourself that love–even when it was hard for you and you don't think you did it perfectly–is another piece of yourself that you get back. It'll be a dirty, starving piece of yourself that you get back. But it's yours and now it's home so you can work on cleaning it, feeding it, and loving it. And voila, your self-worth gets a little boost.

Keep doing this messy work. And keep doing it. And doing it. Abusers, manipulators, and Status Quo Keepers will say, "You didn't handle that well," and that little piece of self-worth you got back will whisper in your ear, "I don't care how you did it, I'm just glad you did." And next time they respond back with, "Well, you're just as bad as me, you yelled at me," your self-worth will whisper a reminder, "It's them or me and I'm glad you chose me."

What no one tells you is that this step in the healing process is messy and embarrassing and *uncomfortable*. But remember, each time you do it you are practicing self-love which is slowly growing your self-worth. And someday, you're going to enter a room walking taller and appearing untouchable. And that, my love, is confidence. Turns out, you didn't need four-inch heels and the strut of a runway model. You just needed to get messy and prove to yourself that you are worth all of the hard things.

Who Invited Self Sabotage?

So, which came first? Self-worth or confidence? Neither. Self-love came first.

Then self-worth.

Then confidence came riding the coattails of your hard work.

Unfortunately, for many of us, you're not done. Something else comes after self-worth and confidence. . .

Once you start building up your self-worth and the life you want, you'll need to keep a watchful eye for self-sabotage. Gay Hendricks, in *The Big*

Leap: Conquer Your Hidden Fear and Take Life to the Next Level, warns us about this hidden side-effect of working hard to get where we want to be. "Each of us has an inner thermostat setting that determines how much love, success, and creativity we allow ourselves to enjoy. When we exceed our inner thermostat setting, we will often do something to sabotage ourselves, causing us to drop back into the old, familiar zone where we feel secure."

Yes, honey, *you* could be the one that ruins *everything*. All your hard work. As you continue working toward healing and other goals in your life, it's important to make sure your body and brain don't try to bring you back down to familiar territory. It's sneaky when it happens!

It is usually some small action that snowballs into something bigger until you're sitting in your living room wondering what the hell just happened. Other times, self-sabotage can manifest in your body. You stand up for yourself at work, you get that raise, and then you injure your foot or knee. I'm not victim-blaming! I swear this is a real thing and you need to be prepared for this! You would not believe how many physical injuries manifest after someone gets what they've been working toward.

For some women, it could mean building up self-worth and then turning around and dating someone when their intuition is screaming to stop. Or could mean losing some weight and then binging pizza and ice cream until you feel like a huge piece of shit. Your body and brain will work *so hard* to bring you back to the status quo. Don't let it!

Focus on how GOOD it feels to have what you've attained. Marinate in those feelings and let them soak into your cells and bones. Tell yourself that you deserve these things. Tell yourself this is your new life now and your new life includes these good things. This good is your new normal. This is the standard and default setting for your life. You won't go lower than this. If you suddenly have more money, look at the numbers in your account and celebrate.

Do this every day if you must! If you're in a good relationship, lay in bed and think about how wonderful this feels. If you're newly single, stand naked in your room and feel the freedom you have. Think about how powerful you are now that no one is sucking energy from your body. Enjoy where you are on this path in life. Bask in the glow. When your brain speaks up and says, "This feeling won't last forever," you reply, "Well, it sure does feel wonderful while it's here and now I know what my standards are."

Being cognizant that self-sabotage could be creeping around the corner is a great way to watch out for your own bullshit. When you level up in one aspect of your life, you might try to sabotage another aspect. You got promoted at work? Ok, don't start fights with your partner or BFF so your brain has *something* to be unhappy about. Stay ready and stand up for yourself and your self-worth when the time comes.

Villain Era Battle Notes

Self love is a battlefield! And building self-worth is done in the trenches while setting boundaries. "Battle notes" contains the plans you have in place as you set boundaries and navigate your villain era. It gives you ap lace to celebrate wins every time you stand up for yourself and helps prepare for discussions around boundaries so you can continue protecting yourself. Grab a piece of paper or visit villaineragoddess.com to download a worksheet that's ready to go!

Self-Love Victories

Start by celebrating your bravery and document the times you've stood up for yourself and your family. Keep adding to the list! This list will help you stay positive as you fight day-to-day battles.

Boundaries and Battle Prep

What boundaries would you like to set to protect yourself and your family?

This can include boundaries with family, school, work, friends, etc. Covering anything from how people speak to you to how family members treat you or your children.

When it's time to set a boundary, what will you say? Write down planned-out responses so you feel prepared for any future altercations. Remember, setting a boundary isn't telling someone they can't treat you a certain way—it's telling them what the consequence is once they do treat you that way. You have to tell people how you want to be treated!

There are a couple of ways to organize your responses to boundary breakers and over-steppers:

Underline: If you have time to have a conversation before the boundary is crossed:

- Be proactive and tell them what you need from them and how you'd like to structure your relationship around this boundary.
- State what you will and won't tolerate in this situation. Give examples.
- Let them know how you'd like to be treated in this scenario.

In the moment, right after the boundary is crossed:

- State what you won't tolerate, pointing out what just happened.
- State the consequence if they continue to do so.
- Stick with it!

Examples of responses when someone is crossing your boundary:

- I feel uncomfortable when my body is the topic of conversation. Please refrain from commenting on my physical appearance or I'll need to leave/report to HR/reconsider this relationship.
- We don't pressure the kids into hugging without their consent. Please don't make them feel bad if they don't want to hug or we won't be able to stop by anymore.
- Damn, that's a personal question! I keep some things sacred and

that's one of them! How about we change the topic?

- That's not funny. I hope your jokes get better because I'd like to continue hanging out.

Boundary responses:

Start planning your response when someone crosses your boundaries!

1. What's the issue? Think of a specific scenario and write that down.
2. Next, write down the boundary you'd like to set.
3. The last step is to write your response when someone crosses the boundary. This will help you prepare!

Stop Your Inner Traitor

Becoming the best version of yourself and living a life that supports that version of you is your birthright. Making subtle and drastic changes to your life as you learn life lessons is your right, and being rewarded for your hard work is your inheritance from the universe. You are worthy of these changes and big moves.

Different Isn't Always Wrong and Familiar Isn't Always Right

When you purposely choose your new standards and stick with them, your version of "familiar" will slowly level up to meet you where you are. Until then, your brain and body might try to bring you back down to the familiar territory you just escaped from. Let's create a game plan so you don't sabotage your own hard work.

Ways we sabotage our progress:

- Putting yourself in tempting situations
- Prioritizing the wrong things
- Procrastination or lack of preparation

- Substance abuse, over-spending, other excessive behavior
- Controlling or micromanaging behavior
- Picking fights or starting conflicts (being defensive)
- Avoiding or withdrawing from others
- Negative self-talk and extreme self-criticism
- Breaking promises and being forgetful

Ways we can support yourself:
- State affirmations to remind yourself of your worth.
- Treat your future self. What gift can you give yourself to support yourself tomorrow?
- Be gentle with mistakes, but firm in not going back.
- Create a plan to help you stop self-sabotage behavior.

Affirmations and Reminders That You're Worthy:
- I am worthy of the good things that happen to me. In fact, I deserve them.
- I release negative thoughts and feelings so I can replace them with something that benefits me and my journey.

Write your own in your journal or download the worksheet at villaineragoddess.com.

👑 *This battle-weary queen-of-calling-fuckers-out who's in the pursuit and preservation of self-worth gives you permission to get messy as fuck as you set boundaries and protect yourself. You have my permission to behave like a rabid honey badger when it comes to guarding the goodness you've created for yourself!*

I'M STRONG ENOUGH TO TEMPORARILY EXCHANGE MY COMFORT FOR A CHANCE AT FREEDOM AND GROWTH WHEN THE TIME COMES.

TOOLS FOR YOUR VILLAIN ERA

12. RITUALS AND ROUTINES FOR VILLAINOUS QUEENS

Glow brighter than the haters.

Stop raw dogging the day and getting triggered on dumb shit.

What do your morning and evening routines consist of?

I'm not talking about starting the dishwasher before bed. I'm referring to morning routines that prepare you for the day and evening routines that restore your mental health before bed.

If you're not careful, then your morning routine might be that you're walking around on autopilot, already checked out before the day begins. Or starting your day in panic mode because you're feeling unorganized. Your evening routine might default to you berating yourself with unproductive, mean thoughts.

Glow and Grow Routine - The Double G's of Self-Care

It's time to create healthy habits with a brand-sparkling-new "Glow and Grow" routine! These aren't just boring everyday habits. These are rituals and practices to ensure you're glowing and growing each day.

Arm Yourself with Protection

These "Glow and Grow" routines are vital for anyone navigating their villain era. You already know about the fuckery that comes with establishing boundaries and protecting yourself and your family as you morph into a villain. That's why it's so important to arm yourself with as many protections as you can. Instead of being reactive like a hissing feral cat, you'll be prepared, stalking through the grass like a cheetah.

Each step in your "Glow and Grow" routine is like putting on pieces of armor to protect yourself. You'll be more equipped to establish habits that:

- supports your physical, emotional, and mental well-being
- reduces stress
- protects your energy
- supports growth

Or the opposite. If you don't consciously create positive routines, then negative habits will take over like zombie garden gnomes, eating your flowers and attacking house guests.

Protect Yourself from ... Yourself

And listen. While fortifying yourself from the bullshit of the outside world is essential, you also need to ***protect yourself from your own bullshit as well***. I probably don't have to tell you that your mind can be a nasty little place from time to time. And battling yourself for no reason, other than you don't have systems in place to stop yourself from spiraling, can leave you feeling out of control and your self-worth in the gutter.

I'm not saying it's easy. My daily routines are the first things I forget about when life feels like I've boarded Amtrak and I'm on my way to peace and contentedness. I'm sitting back like a passenger, enjoying the view. As soon as shit derails, I'm stumbling around wounded and bleeding, wondering how in the hell I'm going to get out of this mess and heal.

Routines for Taking Control

Evidently, I'm the type of person who has to derail in a horribly loud, dramatic fashion before I remember I should have been driving the train, not sitting in the dining car, and should have been following routines and habits to prevent this crap.

Over time, I've learned that I have to stick with my daily Glow and Grows (or Double G's, if you will) if I want an easier life where I can celebrate wins instead of hyper-focus on losses. I have to continually:

- clear my energy
- build myself back up after a tough day
- honor my inner child
- feel my emotions so I can let them go
- take time to show this meat sack of a body some attention.

If I don't, then when I derail—and I totally will—it is in a spectacular fashion with explosives, cannons, creepy clowns, and that cringy carnival music from horror films.

The times in my life when I've made huge strides, I was practicing my Double Gs religiously to get myself in the right headspace. When I was getting ready to quit my job in Corporate America and start my own business, I recited affirmations *all day long*. In the shower, while driving to work, going pee, before bed. It worked! I went from a new business owner with zero guaranteed income to pulling in thousands a month.

In the past, I would lie in bed at night and berate myself for any mistake I made during the day. Or I would overthink conversations. I've since replaced that with an evening routine that focuses on

- celebrating my wins.
- self-care practices.
- meditating on my goals.

As you can imagine, that was a nice switch from my previous practice of literally calling myself a fat, stupid piece of shit before bed. I didn't realize how much negative self-talk I had running on a loop in my head *until I replaced it*!

Your Glow and Grows are such a great way to switch from surviving in stank-ass pond water to thriving in fresh spring water. Examples of routines include affirmations, energy-protection visualizations, taking time to be grateful, stretching and moving your body before bed, reciting an incantation while stirring your coffee, meditation, journaling, sleep-inducing relaxation techniques, and more. By making these habits a part of your daily life, you can better protect your energy and feel more productive and fulfilled.

To get started, you have to decide that you're worth the work it takes to start daily routines and habits. Before I consciously focused on my daily routines, I centered my actions around my family, work, and other obligations. Not around what I needed. Even when I first started saying affirmations each day in the shower before I quit Corporate America, I still didn't understand that I was continuing to center myself around everything but me. I was using the environment outside of myself as motivation. Fulfilling obligations and ensuring your kids are ready for the day *are* important, but they're not the *only* thing you should be focusing on. And certainly not the first thing you should be focusing on if you want to be in the right frame of mind to get through your day.

Glow and Grow Morning Routine

One of the biggest reminders as you get started is that the most life-altering, potent magic is found in your everyday run-of-the-mill actions.

And daily routines are about as run-of-the-mill as you can get! Author Brianna Wiest talks about micro shifts in her book *The Mountain is You*. Micro shifts are tiny increments of change in your day-to-day life. These micro shifts are what move your life in another direction. It's what motivates you to *want* better until you *are* better, and it helps you continue to *stay* better.

Ready to start? Let's add some magic to your morning!

- Say affirmations in the shower or while putting on your makeup (or both).
- Write down or think about 3 things you're grateful for. Not in a positive mood? That's fine, be grateful for plumbing, coffee, and your padded bra.
- Light a candle and follow a light stretching or yoga routine on YouTube. Or do a quick stretch routine while you wait for the coffee to finish brewing.
- Give yourself a facial massage or hit acupressure points while applying your daily moisturizer.
- Think about your goals and dreams and choose one easy, quick thing you can do today to get yourself one step closer to that dream.
- Think about how you want to feel today and then think about one small thing you can do today to usher in that feeling for yourself.
- Picture a sparkly bubble around you, ready to protect you from negative energy.

Glow and Grow Evening Routine

Let's remove the day's energy and open your mind before bed:

- Journal your "wins" for the day. This could include compliments at work or in your personal life, achieving a step toward your goals, or seeing progress from hard work. If you can't think of a win, then write down that you at least opened your journal because that's a win.
- Write down any ideas, motivations, and thoughts for your goals and dreams. Anything you can think of that keeps you excited and moving forward.
- Document your mood for the day. If you want, you can also document anxiety, triggers that came up for you during the day, and anything else you want to keep track of.
- Check your family calendar and your work calendar to make sure you know exactly what's coming up tomorrow. Add reminders in your phone if you're worried you'll forget something. Or keep sticky notes by your bed and jot notes down there so you can reference it tomorrow. Then let it go and leave it for tomorrow.
- Write affirmations or messages on your bathroom mirror with a dry erase marker that you'd like to read first thing tomorrow morning.
- Reflect on how much you've been connecting with others and if you want to make changes to anything. This is a great time to think about friends you haven't seen in a while. Send them a text to see how they're doing or to set up a time to get together.
- Swipe your hands down your body, imagining that you're brushing negative energy off yourself before you get into bed.

I hope you get started tonight! The amazing thing is that those feelings of protection, productivity, and fulfillment will continue to grow as you stick with your routines. Positive life changes don't happen in one moment. It's not one big event that explodes in your face, leaving you glowing, eyes sparkling with joy, smelling like lilacs, and living the life you always dreamed of. I wish! No, those of us stuck on this fricken rock spinning in outer space have to put in the work each day to heal and change. It might not look like progress in that exact moment, but it adds up to big moves in the future.

Build Your Glow and Grow with a Morning Routine

It's time to start creating your own plan! You have more control over your day than you think! This morning routine guide can help you create an environment that ensures your day starts off with encouraging words and positive actions. Use this worksheet to create your own morning routine and CHOOSE how your day is going to go.

Grab a piece of paper or visit villaineragoddess.com to download a worksheet that's ready to go!

Affirmations

List 3 affirmations you're going to say every single day. Incorporate these into your daily routines so they're easier to remember. For example, say them while brushing your teeth, stirring your coffee—whatever works for you.

1.
2.
3.

The goal is to be grateful and make statements like you already have what you want. Stay away from "I want," "I wish," and "I need." Here are examples:

- Financial: Money and opportunities flow freely to me in unexpected ways.
- Confidence: I am worthy of what I desire.
- Romantic Relationship: I am an amazing girlfriend/wife/partner and I'm so grateful for the love I share with my person.
- Family Dynamic: I am grateful for my happy, healthy family.
- Friendship: I am grateful for my wonderful group of friends who I trust and love.
- Career: Opportunities and advancement flow freely to me and it feels amazing.
- Less Stress: I choose my environment and I choose peace.
- Health: I am healthy, I am happy, I enjoy being active and making healthy decisions, I live a life full of abundance.

Rituals

List 1-3 ritual ideas you can quickly add to your morning routine. Rituals are basically just habits with a spiritual vibe.

1.
2.
3.

Ritual ideas include:

- Affirmations in the shower
- Daily mantra while stirring your coffee
- Write down 3 things you're grateful for
- Energy-protection ritual
- Light a candle or incense while you get ready
- Document dreams

Self-Care

List 3 quick and easy self-care ideas you can add to your morning routine to show yourself a little extra love.

1.

2.

3.

Self-care ideas include:
- Facial massage or facial yoga while putting on facial lotion or cream
- Essential oils or perfume on your chest so you can smell it all day
- Enchant jewelry as armor and wear it
- Enchant your coffee cup or travel mug (visit villaineragoddess.com for directions on how to enchant your coffee mug)
- Stretch your body in the shower, while making coffee, or even while laying in bed

Pursue Your Dreams

What are you working on? Are you building confidence and self-worth? Maybe workout goals, career goals, personal goals are your main focus? Write down one goal or dream you're pursuing.

Next, choose one small action today to support your goal and dream. What's one small thing you can do today to help you get one step closer to that goal? Making a list? Sending one text message or email? Parking further from work for a longer walk? Meditating for one minute?

Manage Your Mood

How do I want to feel today? Carefree, confidence, less stress, organized, peaceful, etc. List out or think through one thing I can do to feel that way today. Examples are:

- Commit to joy by approaching 1 task you hate with more positivity today
- Not participating in negative talk at work
- Play relaxing music
- Practice reframing my thoughts

Build Your Glow and Grow with an Evening Routine

This evening routine guide can help you create an environment that ensures your day ends with self-reflection and routines centered in self-love. Use this worksheet to create your own evening routine and CHOOSE how tomorrow is going to go. Grab a piece of paper or visit villaineragoddess.com to download a worksheet that's ready to go!

Daily Reflection

Creating a list of what you'd like to reflect on each day is a big step toward monitoring your own health. It's also a surprising way to show yourself some love because you're taking the time to focus on YOU. Bonus: you'll eventually start to see patterns in your mental and physical health to help you celebrate wins or notice if you have something to work on or see the doctor about.

I prefer to reflect on:

- Wins:
- Goals:

- Mood:

For example:
- Wins: What went well today? Did something go smoothly? Did you get a compliment? Were you proud of yourself?
- Goals: Keep track of progress on current goals as well as list out new goals or ideas you have.
- Mood: On a scale of 1 to 5, how was your mood for the day?
- Other areas of reflection: Water intake, period tracking, anxiety tracking, triggers that came up, etc.

Evening Rituals

Once again, rituals are like habits with a spiritual spin. Use this time to create habits and routines that allow you to check in with yourself and grow as a person. Or just to heal and rest. We don't always have to be chasing self-perfection all the time! List 1 to 3 rituals you can incorporate into your evening routine.

1.
2.
3.

Examples of rituals include:
- Affirmations
- Reading
- Journaling
- Rituals, spells, alter updates
- Shadow work and therapy lessons
- Relaxing yoga or stretching
- Sleep meditation

Self-Care

Hey, you made it through the day! List 3 quick and easy self-care ideas you can incorporate into your evening to give yourself a bit more pampering or to help you end the day on a positive note.

1.

2.

3.

Ideas for end-of-day self-care are:
- Facial massage or facial yoga while putting on facial lotion or cream
- Essential oils on your pillow
- Write a love note to yourself after a hard day
- Teeth whitening, lip exfoliation, lotion on the heels of your feet, etc
- Clear negative energy from your body

Looking at Tomorrow

What big plans do you have tomorrow? Would it be helpful for you to sketch out a plan for how you want your day to go? Look at:

- Family calendar
- Work calendar
- Daily reflections to see if you need a doctor appt, massage appt, etc.

Connecting with Others

If you've been feeling lonely or like you want to start connecting more with others, then take some time to think about how you want that to happen.

How can you connect with others? In a perfect world, how would you connect with your partner, kids, extended family, friends, coworkers, and network connections?

Next, think about who you can connect with. Who can you call or text to start making plans with? Who do you need to catch up with? Any friends you can make a bigger effort with?

List out ideas so you are more prepared to act tomorrow!

I give you permission to show off your Double Gs and gift yourself grace, patience, and unconditional love. I join you in celebrating where you are today with tiny improvements made each day. I give you permission to love yourself no matter what, because you're worth it.

I ACCEPT POSITIVE, HELPFUL THOUGHTS THAT ALLOW ME TO MOVE FORWARD EACH DAY.

13. TOSS TOXIC POSITIVITY IN THE TRASH

Gratitude that feels different.

A fetish, but not what you think.

Chasing "Good Vibes Only" will leave you winded, hands on your knees, gasping for breath and feeling like a loser for not achieving it.

That's because it's a lie. There's no such thing as "Good vibes *only.*" It's ok to chase good vibes, but good vibes *only*? Get the fuck out of here. This is real life. We will kill ourselves chasing fake, hollow vibes if we're not careful.

That said, not focusing on "Good Vibes" and letting your "Inner Grumbler" take over will leave you laying on the floor with a tv remote in one hand and bag of chips in the other, wondering what the hell went wrong. Your Inner Grumbler has one mission in life. To leave you feeling just as miserable today as you were yesterday. Lil Miss Inner Grumbler loves to replace positive thoughts with miserable, loathing, fearful, anxious thoughts instead. Fun, right?

The Inner Grumbler

Do you have an Inner Grumbler? Just grumbling all the damn time. "My shoulders hurt." "I don't want to go to this meeting." "I'm hungry but don't want to cook." "I hate driving to the bank."

I do. She doesn't shut the fuck up. She's the first thing in my head in the morning. She's the last thing I hear at night, going through all the things I did wrong during the day. She sits on my shoulder all day long—while reading email, while going to meetings, while texting my friends. She's right there, ready to deliver negative one-liners that make me want to crawl back into bed.

I've been working very hard on replacing my Inner Grumbler with a more positive version of myself. It's slow going and a constant battle. She's *relentless.* If this sounds familiar, please know that you're not alone. And if you're having a hard time silencing your Inner Grumbler, you're not alone!

Ridding yourself of the Inner Grumbler is a messy, rough road. I argue with mine almost daily. For example, late one night while feeding my TikTok addiction, I came across a video from some lady who is an expert in quantum-something-or-other (her title sounded super cool and very important in understanding the spiritual realm). She was talking about how the *biggest* shift you can make when manifesting your dream life is to change how you wake up.

This is what she said: When you first wake up—the first consciousness of the day—you're supposed to place your hands at your heart center, take four deep breaths, and envision yourself getting up and living your dream life. Like you already have everything you want and you're so grateful for it. You're waking up so blessed. You *know* you're starting your day how you want to start your day, in the house you want, getting ready for the job you want, etc. You *know* you already have it. And you're grateful for it.

This is the *very first thought* you should have of the day.

My Inner Grumbler immediately scoffed at this. At the time I saw this video, my toddler had been waking up yelling for me every day around 5:00 a.m. Every. Damn. Day. 5:00 a.m. She'd wake up pretty pissed off that I wasn't standing by her bed, ready for her to start the day. Every. Day.

My Inner Grumbler reminded me of this and said "Good luck" with a hairflip. She almost won and I almost gave up on this new positive spin before I even started. I mean, how do you wake up feeling blessed when your heart is racing and rage is running through your veins because it's way too early for a kid to be yelling?

I finally wrestled that negative grumbler into submission and pointed out her bullshit. Even though my daughter was waking up as loudly as possible, ready to play and upset we didn't read her mind and stand by her bed to await her first demands of the day, I really was blessed.

Why couldn't I still wake up feeling grateful and blessed? I mean, a screaming child was better than no child. So I was blessed. And I knew she would be out of this phase (hopefully) soon. But I really am blessed and when I picture my perfect life—it doesn't include screaming obviously, but it does include the little stinker who wakes me up.

So I started trying it. It first went like this:

Cue the screaming at 5:00 a.m.

INNER GRUMBLER: Are you fucking kidding me.

ME: You mean, "Aw, our little rainbow baby is up and ready to hang with her mom. Let's go get her. Let's sniff her. I bet she smells like a sleepy toddler."

That's as good as I could do. I could not take the four deep breaths. I have way too much anxiety while my kid screams. But I could at least try to imagine my perfect life while I rolled out of bed, blindly searching for my glasses, letting the dog out of the kennel so she doesn't whine while I grab the toddler. And doing that has to be better than screaming "FUUUUUCK" in my head and allowing dread to fill my body.

It helped! I quickly saw a change in myself as I started doing this. I wasn't always imagining my most perfect life and feeling blessed, but I was waking up feeling grateful for what I had. What I've figured out is that feeling gratitude doesn't mean my life will have any less problems, it's just that solutions come to me faster and with less stress.

Love and Light? More Like Shame and Confusion

I've always struggled with the privileged-based manifestation movement and books like "The Secret" about manifesting your dream life. I felt like they weren't looking at a bigger, more realistic picture. And don't even get me started on how this movement victimizes survivors by telling us we're "asking for it" when something bad happens. Like my two-year-old self manifested hardships because my mindset wasn't right. Gratitude is life changing, but you don't have to do it in a toxic way, and I believe you'll be better off if you follow the original "love and light" movement which is literally just about spreading love and light. Don't get stuck on the new-age manifestation train that makes lots of stops at "You're doing it wrong" station.

When we decide to be more positive and grateful, we sit around waiting for rainbows to start shooting out of everyone's ass, money falling from the sky, and the haters kissing our feet when we walk into a room. That's because you're still recovering from the love and light movement. It's ok. I was like that, too.

But that's not how it works! Your car will still have a flat tire. Your cousin will still text you some shit that pisses you off. Your co-workers will still pull some stunts. But instead of spiraling down and getting stuck in the trenches with your Inner Grumbler, you'll have a clearer solution in your mind and it's easier to implement.

If you've had an Inner Grumbler your entire life, then you might not even realize she's chirping in your ear non-stop. Especially if your parents were grumblers, too. You don't know what the alternative feels like. To you, this probably is living a positive life! But those who don't have Inner Grumblers would like for you to know that you have too much negative talk and you need to calm that shit down.

I Like Big "Buts"

If you're ready to start silencing your Inner Grumbler, I've found the easiest way to get started is to start adding "but at least…" at the end of every negative thought.

For example, "I hate going to meetings" turns into "I hate going to meetings, but at least I know I'm getting paid for this. Cha-ching."

What you say in your head, and especially what you say out loud, has so much impact on how your life turns out.

This is one of the easiest ways to start silencing those negative thoughts. It's very eye-opening, because you'll start to realize how many negative thoughts you have a day based on how many times you're finishing a thought with "but at least."

Gratitude Works, Man

Another tactic that will have a positive impact on your mental health is to start writing down three things you're grateful for every morning. (Go back to the Glow and Grow chapter for a refresher!) Some days are harder than others, and your three things might have been things like: air to breathe, coffee, crocs (hey, I won't judge).

Use this time to check in with yourself as well. Rate your mood each day in your journal, on a scale from 1 to 5. 5 being orgasmic and 1 being found in a ditch.

I was shocked at how I started rating my days at 3.5, 4, 4.5 … and I was having the same type of days. They weren't suddenly amazing days full of ease and laughter. They were the exact same! Arguments with kids, remembering I have to get gas while I'm already running late, running out of coffee, all of those same annoying things. But I was brushing them off and only remembering the highlights at the end of the day. That seems worth 10 minutes of journaling to me!

So, yeah, gratitude sounds cheesy, and way overplayed in self-help books. But it works.

Keep Practicing

If you have an easy time staying positive, then please know I'm so jealous. I'm still working on this, and even when I see positive results in my life, I still have to fight my Inner Grumbler. I will sometimes fall off the wagon and into a ditch (that gets a mood rating of 1). But as soon as I find myself falling into old patterns, I will put a sticky note on my bathroom mirror that says "But at least" and then will get myself back into the habit of being positive.

👑 *I give you permission to talk dirty about those buts. "I hate going to the grocery store, but at least my boobs will look perky in the freezer aisle." You also have all of my permission in the world to write down whatever you're grateful for. At first, you might be grateful that Becky tripped in her hooker heels while acting like a know-it-all at work. Write it down! If you don't start somewhere, then you'll have nowhere to go.*

I'M THANKFUL FOR MY AMAZING LIFE.

14. ACCESS YOUR INNER-GODDESS WITH FREE WRITING

Let your inner goddess loose.

"I said that?" and other thoughts you'll have after free writing.

Do the joints in your body feel like they're going to separate at any moment because you're bursting full of thoughts and energy and emotions and reactions and continually swallowing it all down to wear fake smiles for those around you? And you're not sure if you're going to fall to the floor ugly-crying or jump up and rage scream into your decorative pillows or throw cilantro at strangers in the grocery store?

Healing from trauma while also entering your villain era comes with big, heavy feelings all the damn time. You don't get to hunker down at home and lick your wounds. You have to stand right back up and continue to be the protector and enforcer. Sometimes it can feel like you never get a break. Sure, maybe Tuesday went well, but then Wednesday comes shuffling onto the scene, vaping and causing a ruckus, forcing you to set even more fucking boundaries and recover from being triggered.

Many women I talk to want to avoid this part of the healing process because it's messy and exhausting. We're already working, returning Snapchat messages, running errands, returning text messages, cleaning the house, avoiding phone calls (why won't they just text?), making plans with friends and family, returning Facebook (or is it Meta?) messages, and being too full of everything else that life throws at us. Just thinking about the fact that we have to think about healing from trauma is *exhausting*. Following all the recommended healing techniques is fucking exhausting. Following your therapist's instructions, reading books about healing, watching a YouTube video about healing—it's all fucking exhausting.

That's why I love free writing, because there is literally no structure or rules. And there's a reason why it's included in so many therapies. It works! You will get to know yourself better and become your own best friend, sister, and mother when you start free writing. You will awaken your inner-goddess of guidance, wisdom, and protection. And you will *feel* this shift.

Free writing is a powerful, freeing tool that can help you move forward. It allows you to "go deeper" while journaling by accessing your subconscious to map out ideas, encouragement, and solutions in a safe and private space without fear of judgment or criticism.

Stop the Verbal Vomit

I first started free writing during the new moon because I liked the energy around me at that time. I would usually free write with a theme of moving forward (new moon vibes) which always included thoughts around my healing process, my villain journey, and goal setting in general. It helped me get past my own bullshit and access my inner consciousness. I saw the benefits in so many ways, but one of the biggest benefits was that I stopped spewing all of my thoughts and memories to my poor husband.

One evening I noticed I left the man shell-shocked after telling him a memory that surfaced from my childhood. I wanted to talk it out and who best to do that with than the person who loves me the most? Right? *Wrong!* Just because someone loves you, it doesn't mean they should be forced into your haunted house—this is where I had to unlearn a toxic behavior from my childhood, which is that we get full access to those we love, no matter what. But that's a whole other topic.

Think of your memories and triggers as a haunted house. You wouldn't just shove someone in a haunted house. No, you'd let them make that decision on their own. I realized that by me talking to my husband about every little fucking thing, I was traumatizing him, too. It was actually really selfish of me.

Once I realized what I was doing, I decided I'd journal about any memories or triggers I had instead of verbally vomiting them at my husband's feet, like my dog after eating too much grass. When I was done journaling and documenting the memory, my feelings, and my reactions, I'd then start free writing.

Free writing is less about documenting and more about writing down whatever the hell comes to mind. Journaling is beneficial because it allows you to get the messiness out of your head and on paper, but free writing is *magic* because your subconscious will start delivering lessons and insights you didn't realize you were even storing in the back of your mind.

Another benefit I stumbled onto was realizing that I have great insights! Sometimes it feels like life is happening to you so fast that you don't get to be an active participant the way you'd like. Free writing allowed me to slow down and make plans for jumping into life head-on and actually enjoy it. It allowed me to have more control. This inner-guidance was being drowned out during the day, competing with the mess in my head. Free writing became a powerful tool that was easy for me to access.

And lastly, after free writing for a while now, those healthy "free journal" thoughts and ideas jump through the mess in my head even when

I'm not journaling so I actually notice them when I need them. Not all the time, but enough to notice that I'm growing and getting stronger mentally. It was free writing that woke up my inner self, and right now she's just kind of stretching and learning she can take up space again. I'm excited for the day when she takes over 100 percent. Free writing is a gift in that it can help promote self-awareness, reduce stress, improve creativity, boost your mood, and enhance problem-solving skills. Yeah. Kinda nice, huh?

How to Free Journal

Free journaling is an exercise to help you calm your mind and listen to your intuition. Think of it as an informational download from your soul. Release everything your soul would like to tell you that is held in all day while you survive a busy schedule, family routine, depression, anxiety, fear, and everything in between.

You will need:
- Music
- Timer
- Candle
- Paper or journal
- Pen or pencil

Tips:
- Don't overthink this or judge yourself. Just write down what comes to mind.
- Ensure you won't have any distractions during this exercise.
- It's ok if it starts off rocky with single words or colors coming to mind at first. Write it all down.
- Write down intrusive thoughts to get them out of your mind so you can get back to free journaling from the soul.

Directions:

1. Find a place where you won't be interrupted.
2. Put on relaxing music.
3. Set a timer on your phone for 10 minutes.
4. Light a candle.
5. Close your eyes and take 5 deep, slow breaths. As slow and deep as you can manage.
6. Sit with your hands in your lap. Feel your body relax. Feel your mind paying attention to your body and how it's relaxing. Notice your ears hearing the music. Notice your breathing. Be in the present moment.
7. Open your eyes and look at the candle. Act like you're breathing in the energy of the candle's flame and breathing out any messiness, anxiety, or negative thoughts with 5 more deep, slow breaths.
8. Keep your mind focused on your intentions for a couple of breaths. Those intentions could be to release fear, work through a trigger, discover why you feel the way you do something or someone, map out your future, remove blocks from your past, whatever comes up for you!
9. Look down at your paper and start writing the first thing that comes to mind.
10. Write until the timer goes off.
11. Read through your journal entry when the 10 minutes are over to see what kinds of messages you've given yourself.

👑 *I give you permission to tap into your inner goddess by pouring yourself a La Croix or whatever your favorite beverage is, lighting a candle, turning on some mood music, grabbing a pen in your favorite color, and then writing whatever the fuck comes to mind. No matter how wild it is. Even the most random shit. Do it.*

I HAVE AMAZING INTUITION, WISDOM, AND AN INNER-GUIDANCE SYSTEM BUILT ON LOVE AND TRUTH.

15. FROM "MEAN TIME" TO "ME TIME"

Mindfulness and meditation.

Unless you're just really into mind-fucks, I'd recommend taking some Me Time for your brain.

Before you strip down naked, standing in the fog next to a roaring ocean, screaming into the abyss until you lose your voice, I'd like to tell you about another way you can tell the world to fuck off (while keeping your clothes on). And that's through mindfulness and meditation.

If you go to bed at night disappointed, feeling like you're stuck on the hamster wheel of life and that each day is just a repeat of the day before, or if you feel rage bubbling up from your stomach and you're scared of how it's going to burst out of your body, then you need to start giving yourself more breaks. Like, a lot more breaks.

Especially when you're in your villain era and you're not just dealing with everyday bullshit, you now have to deal with being the "bad guy" when you set boundaries and you have to plan out tough conversations. It's overwhelming! And each day feels like more crap piling up. A safe way to get off that hamster wheel is to practice mindfulness and meditation.

Mindfulness is easy to get started with and you can do this today. Being mindful literally just means taking a moment to just enjoy what's in front of you for a few moments. It's that simple, but it has big benefits.

I promise you will never regret taking a few moments to enjoy what's in front of you. You can start by noticing the moon, the clouds, and the sun. But then let's get detailed. Watch your coffee or tea swirl in a circular motion after stirring it. Check on your plants to see if there's new growth. Watch the water slide over your hands when you're washing them. Pay attention to how a hot drink or an ice cold drink slides down your throat. Rub your toes or fingers along a soft blanket before getting out of bed.

Mindfulness is such a wonderful way to tell the world and the future and the past to go fuck themselves while you have some Me Time. You're focusing on you and what's in front of you for a bit. Everything else can wait.

By giving yourself these moments, you open your heart and mind up to receiving new information, new thoughts, new creativity, more appreciation and having overall new approaches to life. This is how you get off the hamster wheel!

It starts small, like practicing mindfulness by checking on your plants and talking to them. Then suddenly you're learning how to grow medicinal herbs and instead of life repeating itself over and over, you're now in your backyard, surrounded by nature and bees and birds and roly-poly bugs, harvesting herbs that you'll turn into tea and... wait, who the fuck are you now? Who is this new person with new passions? You'll be pleasantly surprised.

Meditation takes this a step further. Meditation can stop a panic attack, it can stop shame spiraling, it can strengthen you mentally and can even help with sleep. The biggest benefit to meditation and why we should ALL do it is because it helps you re-wire your brain. It's easy to shrug off meditation when someone tells you "it brings happiness"… Well, so does shopping and alcohol. The difference is that alcohol, drugs, and other coping mechanisms give you happiness for a very short amount of time and then you feel worse. Whereas meditation gives you happiness and peace for longer periods of time while also patching the broken parts of your brain that's constantly leaking negative thoughts, which is a long-term fix that benefits you forever.

In *Becoming Supernatural*, Dr. Joe Dispenza talks about how we can "knock our bodies out of normal physiology just by thinking about an all-too-familiar past or trying to control an unpredictable future." So if we can ruin our day with our thoughts, then we sure as hell can uplift our day with our thoughts. If your default is to wake up and say, "Uhhh, I know work is going to be miserable today," then you are waking up every single day predicting your future and unfortunately, when we start predicting our own futures, we make it happen. So your day is going to be shitty. You've focused on how shitty it's going to be since you woke up, and that's what you're going to get. A shitty day. Your default means it's a habit for you. So meditation now needs to be a habit for you. But this is a good habit, because it's going to fix your brain and give yourself a happier life.

The hardest part is finding out which forms of meditations work best for you. Failed attempts at meditation can make you feel like a big loser. Instead of stress lifting off your shoulders, it feels like rage was *added on top of the stress* that was already on your shoulders. Don't give up! Just keep trying new things. I guarantee it works and can take you from stabby to smiley in no time.

I found that I need guided meditations in order to stay focused and calm. I had tried the meditations with just music and kept finding myself frustrated and not feeling calm one bit. I had to reframe my thinking of meditation and tell myself that it's ok to use a guided meditation. Sure, there are tons of people out there talking about their meditative practices that involve nothing except them and a floor. Well, good for them, but I need something that works for me. So guided meditation it is! And I'm glad I did it. This has been a great way for me to dedicate time to reframing thoughts and focusing on the good instead of the bad. I use guided meditations when I'm inside, for example I really enjoy the "I am enough" Guided Meditation by Marisa Peer.

I've also found that I need to add outside stimulation to help me stay present in my body. Yes, it sounds crazy. But I've found that even just a heating pad on my chest and stomach will help ground me into the moment and I can focus on how the heat feels on my skin. When I'm in full-blown, freak-out, panic mode where my clothes can't touch my skin, my hair can't touch my face or neck, and I can't handle *any* noise above a ten decibel level then I need to get a bit more aggressive in staying mindful and present in my body. In walks my acupressure mat.

If you've never seen an acupressure mat, then let me introduce you to my favorite torture device. It is a small mat—about the size of an average person's back—and it's filled with little spikes. The spikes poke into your skin and the first few times you use it, you'll want to scream "What in the actual fuck!" because it hurts like hell. But by the third time? Pure bliss, baby. This mat shuts off all thought as soon as I lay on the little pokies. I often fall asleep while laying on it.

I know others who have to practice breathing techniques for the first ten to fifteen minutes of the meditation in order for it to work. You just have to find what works for you! When I'm dealing with anger, I will use "alternate nostril breathing" and take 10 deep breaths. The calming effect is almost immediate. I'd say by my fifth breath my shoulders drop, my heart rate slows down, and I start feeling better. Begin by sealing your right nostril and take a deep inhalation through your left nostril. Hold that breath while you then seal your left nostril and exhale through your right nostril. In through the left, out through the right. Follow this sequence for as long as you need to. Some people will block 5 to 10 minutes to practice this style of breathing.

Meditation is still a journey for me, but I'm far enough along to have found a routine that helps me stay in the moment while meditating. I'm not yet to the place where I sit in silence for thirty minutes and get up feeling like I could take on a college-level mathematical equation while bench pressing a truck and offering empathy to the biggest bitch I know. Nope. Not there yet. And I'm ok with that. I've found that the secret is to accept that I might not ever be fully enlightened like the monks in the movies and that's ok. I just need to survive, be healthy, and be a good human.

Visit villaineragoddess.com for a list of guided meditations that I can't live without.

I give you permission to give this busy world the middle finger by taking a few minutes to yourself to be completely in the moment.

I'M WORTH AT LEAST FIVE MINUTES.

16.   TURN HOME INTO *HOME*

Create a safety-bubble sanctuary.

"If these walls could talk" ... well, honey, mine actually do.

Do you crave the feeling of "home" even when you're already at home? For years I felt like I was searching for "home" even while I was in my pajamas, sitting on my couch, watching my tv, and eating my own microwave popcorn like I owned the place (I did). I struggled to let my guard down. I didn't feel like it was my space, and I was always a visitor.

Those who've survived tumultuous childhoods can struggle with feeling settled or safe even in their own homes. I was thirty-six years old when I realized that I couldn't remember the last time I'd slept with my back toward the bedroom door.

To feel safe enough to sleep, I needed the door locked *and* to face the door so I could quickly open my eyes to see who was walking in. I wouldn't allow myself to fall into a deep sleep before knowing where everyone in the house was and if they were asleep or not.

This realization came after moving in with my partner. One summer afternoon, I woke up from a nap with blankets wrapped around me like a cocoon, my dog snuggled against my legs, and the afternoon sun sneaking into the room through the sides of the blackout curtains. I was at total peace. I stretched, reached over, and lazily ran my fingers through the curly, tangled fur of my little poodle-dachshund fur baby and then sat straight up with a startling realization. I had fallen asleep with my back to our open bedroom door. The door was WIDE open. But I had slept hard. I sat there wanting to sob uncontrollably, and it took me a minute to figure out why. This is what "safe" felt like! *I was home.* I wasn't sure if I wanted to celebrate the moment or mourn the loss of not having this feeling for thirty-six years.

How did I finally get here?

Two big changes:

1. Creating the safety of "home" within myself while ensuring my outside environment was the fortress I needed to feel safe.
2. Using witchy practices to wake my house up and turn my physical home into a living entity.

Creating Home within Yourself

When our homes don't feel like home, it can prevent us from healing. Robbing us of a safe place to let our guard down. "Home" is the one place where we get to be ourselves, we get to journal with tears in our eyes, we get to snort-laugh as loud as we want to, we get to listen to the same song over and over because it's comforting, we get to try out a new exercise routine that leaves us gasping for air as we flail around like newborn giraffes (or is that just me?). Home isn't where the heart is, it's where the *soul* is.

Creating a safe, relaxing environment is a great way to support your boundaries and protect yourself. This is so important as you do your internal work. When you set the intention that your house is going to be a safe haven for you and your family, it forces you to get clear on what you will and will not accept from those around you and you will be choosy about who enters your home.

As adults, we have what it takes to provide a safe environment for ourselves. We just need the tools to get there. This feeling of home needs to come from inside us. The good news is that it will eventually while we work to heal ourselves. Also note, to get here I had to make sure only safe people could enter my home. I have a list of who isn't allowed in my house. The bad news, if you don't feel safe around your partner, then this will be hard to achieve. I will not tell you what to do in this situation, but this is an area for self-reflection!

While a true home isn't so much a physical location, but a state of being, there are changes you can make to your actual dwelling to increase your feelings of protection and control and to provide a low-stress environment that allows you to focus on healing yourself and supporting your family.

To create a fortress fit for a villain guarding the precious treasures in her home, you'll need to "claim" your house as an extension of yourself. You can do that by setting new house rules, giving your home a personality, and by waking up the energy of your home.

I recommend starting by personalizing your home so you can sit on your couch, lay in bed, soak in the tub, cook dinner, fold laundry, and go to bed at night while feeling like you're in a protective bubble of paradise.

This isn't about buying a landscape painting that looks like it originally hung in a Roadside Motel to decorate your home. We need to first go a bit deeper than just home décor.

Set New House Rules

Put the chore chart down. We're not focusing on rules regarding how often laundry should get done, how long a dish can sit in the sink before it goes into the dishwasher or if you should clean your toilets on Sundays or Wednesdays.

We're focusing on the "hidden" rules, the unseen expectations that can make or break trust. These rules are designed to create a safe place for healing, protection, communication, and resilience. Ask yourself:

- How will you handle mistakes? How will you support growth?
- How will you foster open communication?
- How will you initiate hard conversations?
- How will you offer physical, mental, and emotional protection?
- What does a "safe environment" look like for your family?
- What rules would have helped you grow in a safe environment as a child?

We have four rules in our house that we try to live by:

1. We get to start over fresh every day, and each day is a new chance to do better. This allows my kids and partner to know that the next morning they can expect me to greet them like normal. I'm not going to give them the silent treatment or let a grudge fester and hurt our family even more. And they will do the same for me. (Psst, this is a great rule to force open communication. If I don't want to wake up pissed off at my partner tomorrow, then I better sit down and do hard work with him before bed tonight).

2. We are allowed a safe space to open up about hard, weird, embarrassing, emotional things with level heads. We've got kids with growing bodies, we've got adults who want to try new things, we've got people who are constantly morphing. We need to discuss these new things! We have a system in our house where the kids can text, email, or leave me a letter for anything they're too embarrassed to ask to my face. I will reply in the same manner and not bring it up in person until they're ready.

3. We believe everyone and will listen to their story. Whatever information you share with me, I will believe you. Someone bullying you, picking on you, hurting you? Tell me. I'll believe you. Did I hurt you? Tell me. I'll believe you.

4. We're allowed to call out bullshit but must allow an apology and a way to learn. Am I hovering too much? Did I ask you to do something you think is unfair? Did I pull a selfish move? Call me out. But also allow me to apologize and learn how to fix it. Don't ask me to fix it, show me how to fix it. Because if I'm making the mistake, I'm probably not going to see how to fix it right away!

Think about the values and energy you want to be surrounded with. Do you want to ensure everyone in your house has the freedom and safety to heal and follow their own journeys? Then create it!

Keep adjusting your rules, re-defining them, and getting more specific with the details as you move forward. You're going to love what you come up with. I promise!

Give Your Home a Personality

You want your home to feel like an old friend when you walk through the door. Or if you're like me, you might want your home to feel like a Mother Earth loving, incense-burning, jingle-when-she-walks crone wearing a flowing dress stuffed full of fresh herbs, crystals, and feathers, who opens her arms wide with the excitement of a loving grandmother who welcomes you home every time.

When thinking about your home's personality, ask yourself:

- If your house was a person, what would their vibe be?
- What would their name be?
- What are they into?

- How do they show love to you?

When thinking about the vibe, ask yourself:
- What do you want to smell when you walk into your house?
- What do you want to see when you walk into your house?
- What do you want to see when you walk into and out of your bedroom?
- What do you want to see while you're cooking breakfast?
- What do you want to see while you're showering?

When thinking about your home protecting you, ask yourself:
- What does "safe haven" mean to you?
- How do you want your house to protect you?
- What services can your house provide?

For me, it's a place where I can lay down my fears and anxiety and just be myself. It's a place where my kids are allowed to be messy humans and start over fresh each day. I want my kids to be able to let go of fears and pressure.

Some changes we made to our house after doing this exercise:
- We try to bring natural elements inside. We like using plants as home décor instead of paintings and pictures. We run fountains and diffusers because we like the smell but also like to hear the water bubbling.
- We have whiteboard markers in the bathroom so we can write encouraging messages on the mirror.
- We burn incense or run a diffuser with essential oils every day.
- We bought holiday lights on sale in January to continue the warm, festive, twinkle-light feel all year long. We have fairy lights hidden throughout the house that we can turn on in the evening.
- We want our home to feel like a vacation home at all times—this includes our backyard. Spring through fall, we have a fire going in

our fire pit almost every day, any time of day. We add herbs and incense in our fires to add an extra element. We have solar lights in the yard along the privacy fence and around the patio. We have herbs growing around the patio and our hammock brushes up against the mint during the summer months, giving off the most incredible scent.

- We want to live like we're having company over every day. Get out the good dishes, put on the fun music, light a candle, turn on the fairy lights, put the pretty hand towels in the kitchen, all of the things!

Wake Up the Energy of Your Home

Life is an overwhelming shitstorm with debris flying all over the place. And the dwelling that you picked out to be your shelter from the storm has already been doing hard work for you, even if you haven't seen it yet. It's important to protect, celebrate, and connect with your house, so in return, it can support you and communicate with you.

This sounds far-fetched, but it's true! Your home is more than just an extension of yourself. It's a living entity who should be treated like any other member of your family. There's a saying, "if these walls could talk" . . . Well, they can and they know everything that's going on inside your house. Your home has an amazing amount of energy that you can tap into. All you need to do is wake it up.

My home talks to me all the time. It's like an undercurrent running through the walls and floor. I'm given warnings when I need to check on one of my kids. I know the moods of people in my home as soon as I touch the doorknob of the front door. I can monitor someone's energy better once they're standing in my house. There are people who can't even walk into my house, it's so well protected. It sounds wild—and it is! This gift from the universe is formed in nature. It's a wild energy that's soaking into your walls and is ready to be used. It's the same energy and protection that all animals get to help them protect their homes. We must accept, hone it, and then actually use it.

Ready to wake your house up and introduce yourself? Here are some easy ways to get started today:

- Greet your home when you enter.
- Say "goodbye" and "thank you" when you leave.
- Talk to your house.
- Interact with your house. For example, ask it to help you find missing items (thank it when you're done!).
- Cleanse the energy of your home periodically with herb smoke or spray

As you get to know your house over the next few weeks:

- Hang charms or bells on your front door to honor the sacred space.
- Show your home love while completing daily chores. Instead of grumbling about cleaning, be grateful that you can show your majestic dwelling some love.
- Build mini altars around the home to show appreciation for your home and to help it work for you. This could be adding rose quartz to the bathroom for a boost of self-love while getting ready for the day. It could be bringing in live potted herbs, like basil, that have protective qualities and can also be used in cooking.
- Set up a protection ward that sits inside your home.
- Sprinkle salt outside under windows and door frames to add another layer of protection.

Listen to your intuition as you start to show your home more love and start waking it up. Your home will quickly tell you what it wants. Here are fun ways to connect with your home each month:

Monthly Ideas to Connect with Your Home

January

Start the year off fresh by purifying your home with smoke from dried herbs or incense. Try sage, lavender, cedar, rosemary, sandalwood, or frankincense. Move from room to room to cleanse your sacred space.

February

Choose one room to declutter and release stagnant energy. Light a green candle when you're finished to welcome in new energy and opportunities during Imbolc.

March

Celebrate Ostara by mixing up a spring tea blend using 2 parts mint, 1 part fennel, 1 part ginger, and 3 parts green tea. Drop a freshly cleaned rose quartz stone at the bottom of your cup for extra self-love and sit in a spot where you can enjoy the company of your own home.

April

Start herb seeds indoors to get ready for planting season. Write down a dream you want to achieve on a piece of paper and bury it at the bottom of the herb pot. This includes your house in your dreams and desires. Let your goals grow in your house or backyard with the herbs.

May

Hang ribbons on your front door in the colors of orange, yellow, blue, and purple to represent fire for Beltane. Run your fingers over the ribbons when you walk in the door to release bad energy.

June

Create an outdoor oasis to celebrate the arrival of summer. Add flowers, a fire pit or candles, bright pillows, twinkle lights, incense, fun cups and plates, and anything else that makes your heart sing!

July

Continue celebrating summer and bring the vibes inside your home by building an altar in your home. Create a spiral of circles out of stones, place a candle in the middle of the spiral. Enhance with flowers and trinkets you're attached to.

August

Get ready for the fall months with a mood-boosting tea blend. 2 parts mugwort, 1 part mint, 0.5 parts nettles, 1 part chamomile, 1 part ginger, and 1 part fennel. Enjoy your drink while soaking in the bath or reading a book. The point is to let the cozy, serine vibes ooze out of your body and into your walls.

September

Help the critters in your backyard celebrate Mabon and Autumn Equinox by building a bug hotel for everyone who needs help surviving the winter. Bug hotels are great for apartment decks, too!

October

Honor your ancestors and invite them into your home for a silent dinner on Samhain. Set your table, placing food and drink out for each ancestor you want to invite.

November

Conduct a full moon ceremony to help you release family expectations and cut energetic cords as you enter the holiday season and set boundaries to protect you from family drama. Cutting cords is a great activity before setting boundaries on who can enter your home during the holidays.

<u>December</u>

Create a simmer pot to celebrate Yule and the holiday season. Fill a large pot with water, heat to boiling and add cinnamon sticks, star anise, clove, orange slices, rosemary sprigs, and cranberries. Lower heat to medium after it starts boiling. This also adds some extra moisture to your home if you're in a part of the world that has dry winters.

Since starting the activities in this chapter, I've become fiercely protective of my home. I've claimed this home as my own, setting boundaries and rules, while filling it with items that increase our quality of life. It is truly a sacred dwelling that everyone in my family looks forward to entering. It's the end of a journey full of comfort and peace. And it's the beginning of a journey, helping you prepare for the outside world.

While you get started, please remember that not having a safe home when you were growing up is not your fault. Not providing a safe home for yourself when you were in survival mode is not your fault. Struggling to understand how to provide a safe home for yourself when you have no reference guide is not your fault. This is all a normal progression.

That's why I like these activities so much. It gently ushers you into boundaries around your home and who enters it. It gently ushers you into new boundaries around how people are treated inside your home. With those new boundaries can come many expected—and a lot of unexpected—changes that assist you on your journey. Plus, it gives you more control over your environment and situation, which we can all agree is what we're after.

I give you permission to create a caring, inquisitive, passionate, creative, spontaneous-laughter-inducing, cozy, playful, affectionate, honesty-driven environment that's so protected and secure you'll want to strip naked, blare lo-fi rap music and dance until you fall down. Or until it's time to start dinner.

IN THIS HOUSE, WE START OVER FRESH EACH DAY.

GODDESS LEVEL
UNLOCKED

17. YOU'RE A GODDESS AND THE MATRIARCH

You run the show now.

Do you know your place? Or do you <u>know</u> your place?

You've probably heard this before and if you're like me, you weren't applying it to your life either. So, I'm going to say it again. *When you look for love, safety, and support* outside *of yourself, you will always be disappointed.* Always.

Most people attribute this advice to romantic love, but it's relevant to all types of love. I'd say it's probably more important to first apply this to family relationships if your childhood played out like a psychological thriller.

How do family dynamics start? When do kids pick up on it? I think it starts when you're very young and you hear an adult summarize a situation that involved you and you hear them lie. You think, *That's not what happened*, or *That's not what I said* and you realize there's a narrative happening around you that isn't truthful. You're collateral damage in the narrative that a family member came up with.

I learned early on that the women in my family couldn't be counted on, but I still wanted them to. I still wanted to turn to them for advice and help, and this led to years of heartbreak.

When I look back, I see a very clear path of how I fit into the family and what my role was. These incidents in my childhood served as a constant reminder that I wasn't worthy of a truthful narrative. And each time it was a reminder that I should *never, not even once* speak out. My role was to *endure.*

The Day I "Learned My Place"

I remember being ten years old and having my unstable aunt (who is probably sitting at home with a tinfoil hat on right now) grab my arm during a "fun-filled" family vacation. She pulled me to her and said, "I heard you don't like me and don't like being around me." I *hated* being around her. She filled me with so much anxious energy, and it felt like at any moment she would snap and I'd be her target. She was a dark-sky tornado and cold-thick monsoon rolled into one, waiting to be unleashed and cause destruction. She was constantly surrounded by a feral, vicious energy that sent me scrambling every time.

On this particular trip, I made the mistake of confiding to my grandmother that I wasn't looking forward to seeing this aunt and I didn't want to be around her. When my aunt pulled me aside, I stood there, frozen. Completely shocked and frozen. My grandma! My fucking grandma, who told me I was beautiful and special and her favorite. She betrayed my trust and told my aunt as soon as she walked in the damn door! I was stuck spinning in time and space as my heart splintered into a million pieces. I couldn't breathe. My grandma didn't choose me! She didn't choose to protect me. I did what all good girls do. I put on the brightest, biggest smile and said, "What? Oh, that's not what I meant!" and I *ran*. It was a horrible lie. Everyone knew that was exactly what I meant.

That day was a big day for me. I lost my grandma. Not in the physical sense. She was living and breathing. I lost another person I could trust. And *I learned my place*. The family dynamics were explained to me, in excruciating detail, through my grandmother's actions.

Dear reader, my grandma was my everything. She was my safe space. The loss left a gaping wound that just continued to get bigger and bigger as she kept choosing abusers and bullies over me each and every time throughout my childhood. She just needed for me to be a "good girl" and stay quiet. And maybe that was why she treated me like a favorite. I learned my place pretty quickly, and I continued to serve that role with a gaping wound in my chest.

That wasn't the only incident. Here's the thing with kids. They swallow down the hurt and abuse and try again later. Kids are resilient. Even the "problem kids" are resilient. Their resiliency is in trying to take control over and over again as shit piles on.

I think technically, my role in the family dynamics, crafted by the elders, has never been changed. I was assigned the role of "smile and deal with it" even as an adult. I quickly figured out that no one was really listening to my boundaries and family members would just lie to get what they wanted out of me to continue their own narrative.

I'm still supposed to play that same role. I just choose not to anymore. As an adult, I could finally do something about all of the lying and manipulation that surrounded me. After the second time of showing up to a family gathering that was supposed to be "safe" family members only and seeing that the abusers were in fact invited, I knew I was done. There wouldn't be a third time for me. No one ever told me because they knew I wouldn't come if the "un-safe" people were invited. Worse. No one told me because they knew I wouldn't come *with my kids*. And they wanted to see my kids.

I chose instead to have my own family of people I trusted. I set up my own dynamics and I'm the matriarch.

It's Time to Take Your Place Where You Belong

As you start healing, you're going to want your mom, your sister, your grandma. You're going to want the women in your life who you assume have gone through what you're currently going through.

You'll want comfort, guidance, protection, and most importantly, to be told your feelings are valid, your actions are righteous, and someone has your back. But not all of us will get that. And, if you're reading this book then you probably already know this truth.

You already have doubts that the women in your family will back you up. Support that is crafted from inside a toxic family dynamic will weaken you instead of strengthening you. If your family is codependent, doesn't believe your stories, is narcissistic, or they're just trying to survive the mess in their own heads, then you're not going to get the support you need. *You must provide that support to yourself.*

My mom managed to rebel against certain roles and ideals from her childhood, and I'm grateful for witnessing the inner strength she used when it came to being different from her family. Even through childhood turmoil, I know it could have been worse. I know this because not all of her siblings took the path she did. She broke away and took a few more steps forward from her family based on how she felt internally. And that set me up for better success than some of my cousins who are dead, in jail, or not invited to family events because of their behavior.

My mom took a different route because her intuition told her something was wrong with how she was raised. My goal is for women to do this intentionally in all aspects of their lives. To become their own matriarch with their own rules. When it was my time to heal, I had to take even more steps further from my mom and become my own matriarch. It doesn't mean she's a horrible person, it means she delivered me to a place where I can now continue on my own.

You have to be your own sister, too. This was hard for me. I used to have a very weird, toxic relationship with my sister because I kept waiting for her to step up and be a big sister to me. It took me *years* to realize that she *couldn't* and it took me even longer to realize that she was so traumatized from our childhood and her role in *protecting me* actually caused more abuse toward her when we were kids. By stepping up to be the big sister I needed, I was eventually able to step up and be the big sister that she needed, too, and offer the love and support we were both longing for.

My biggest lesson during this time is: don't be scared to step up to be your own mom, sister, grandma to yourself. You'll be amazed at what you can salvage from some relationships and how easy it'll be to walk away from other unsafe relationships.

Save Your Inner Child by Being the Mom

Women who have survived tumultuous childhoods are left with emotional, physical, and psychological wounds that create their inner voice, create how they see themselves and how they move about the world, and create their list of fears in life. Being your own mom and sister can help you start to turn feelings and narratives around. Loving your inner child and working to change your inner voice is one of the best gifts you can give yourself.

So it's time. This is a big step into your villain era. This step isn't celebrated by others in your family, and it might feel lonely as you get settled in with taking over the roles of mom and sister, but I promise you'll come out the other side stronger and surprisingly with more love toward your family. Get through that transition and you'll get to experience what it's like to start building your own family dynamics in this new role of yours and you build a space that's nurturing and safe for you and your family. The steps after that are inspiring and validating as you and your family *thrive* in this new dynamic.

Since doing this, I'm much closer to my sister and we have both moved into a stage of our relationship where we just want to maximize the love and support we have for each other while we're with each other. By claiming my role as "matriarch" I've been able to guide my mom into a relationship that we both can enjoy. She still worries about me and tries to take control as any mom would but knows that I'm navigating life the way I need to. This didn't happen overnight! There is an uncomfortable transition phase, but the work is worth it!

If you're scared, just remember... What's the alternative? Do you want to sit next to someone you know is an abuser or manipulator, pretending all is well, with your hands shaking and your heart racing? Do you want to feel unworthy of good things because abusers fed you line and line of gaslit bullshit? Do you want to continue adding fear, anger, and shame to your body instead of laughter, joy, and contentment? Do you want to swallow down rage with a huge smile that kills you inside? Do you want to keep following someone else's orders?

Swallowing down your emotions in order to continue playing your role in messed up family dynamics will absolutely block your healing progress. Deciding to be your own matriarch and creating your own family full of healthy dynamics is terrifying when the outcome means you'll be ostracized from the only family you've known. Please listen when I tell you that freedom is on the other side of this decision.

As the mom, the sister, and the matriarch, I can look back at my childhood with maturity and empathy. I look back and see a strong girl who tried to stand up for herself a few times throughout her childhood. She kept trying to grab an adult's attention to get help. That's a strong kid. I'm proud of her. The adults let her down. But guess what. I won't let her down. She's under my protection now and I'm fiercely protective.

The Saving Grace of "Me First"

Grab your villainous crown made of antlers and thorns because becoming the matriarch of your family begins with this thought:

"Me first."

Not "me first" as in being selfish or not sharing. "Me first" as in every decision goes through your gut reaction, your intuition, your objective review. You're probably used to waiting for guidance. You're probably waiting for opinions. You're probably waiting for the guilt trip. All of these tactics are used to push you into a situation that fits the role they designated for you and supports their narrative.

That stops. You're the matriarch. They can now wait to hear from you. That means you hand down decisions to your own mother, your grandmother, your aunts, your sisters and brothers. You are the matriarch of your family. What you say goes.

Some families have a matriarch based on age, others based on who has the most money or who has the most successful job. Do not let this discourage you. You can clean toilets for a living (and if you do—thank you!) or you could be living in a homeless shelter. None of that is the point. You don't need money or material success to be worthy of being a matriarch. You need courage, strength, and the feeling of being so fucking over all the bullshit that you're standing up and getting loud, no matter what. That's what qualifies you.

Honor Yourself

Take time to honor yourself and your journey. This is going to sound wildly egotistical, but you need to build a shrine to yourself, the matriarch of your family. Your shrine is your reminder of who you are, what you've been through, where you're going, and most importantly your reminder that you are unstoppable.

Your shrine could be a crown that you design yourself and set on a shelf. It could be a figurine of a goddess. It could be a gorgeous vase that you fill with flowers once a week to remind yourself of your worth. When someone talks down to you, you can look them in the eye knowing you got a whole-ass shrine built to celebrate your amazing power and they can lower their damn voices when they speak to a goddess. Promise me that you'll build one for yourself!

I give you permission to step out of the shadows and crown yourself matriarch. You'll be made to feel like a selfish, inexperienced, ungrateful child who can't be trusted to make good decisions. That's ok. You already know who you are. You let them call you all the names and make all the assumptions. It doesn't matter anymore. They have no hold over you.

I RUN THIS SHIT.

18. ACCEPTING LIFE AS IT IS

Living easy takes hard work.

If you're going to hate your life, at least do it in party-mode.

I once read that our pursuit of happiness is what makes us unhappy, keeping us feeling unfulfilled. I hated how much that resonated with me. I didn't want to believe it, but deep down my inner Ashley pursed her lips, flipped her hair, and sneered, "I knew it."

Back then I wanted to believe that I could find full-time, always-there happiness. Once found, I'd be floating on cloud nine for the rest of my life.

Instead, I found myself clinging to cloud two with a bunch of other confused people, wondering if this was it for us. I wanted to be a "glass-half-full" kind of girl, but usually just found myself sitting there wondering why we were talking about the glass and weren't just finishing the damn drink.

Finish the Drink

And then it dawned on me. That was the path to happiness. Finishing the damn drink. Metaphorically. I'm not pushing a drinking habit (unless it's lemon-cucumber water, then get after it).

Looking back on my short forty-some-years, the best moments weren't huge moments. They were tiny. Like the smell of baby feet. Or when the sun is shining into your hotel room and you know the beach is right outside. Or the feel of a cat's purr when they're lying on your chest. Or the way your friend's eyes light up before they say something hilarious. Those are the times we finish the damn drink.

Make a pact that today you're going to drink it all in, every time. Especially when you're feeling too busy. I'm not above starting a fire outside in the fire pit on a school day before we leave. Why not sit outside for ten minutes and enjoy something we'd usually reserve for the weekend?

Get out a piece of paper and write down the fun things you make yourself wait for. Things for weekends or vacations. Next to those things, write down how you can incorporate them into your everyday life. Tape this list to your forehead so you don't forget.

I have a running list in the back of my journal and when I feel too overwhelmed to appreciate my life, I pull the list out and remind myself of the fun things I can do right at this moment to drink it all in.

For me, it usually means getting back in the moment and being mindful instead of living inside my head. My family is literally at my fingertips, ready to engage with me and have fun. I have to appreciate them and notice them first. They're ready to drink it in with me. I just need to slow down and join in.

Hate Yourself with Gratitude

Ok, keep reading before you react. You can hate yourself with gratitude.

How? You might ask, because I sound totally unhinged and you can't believe you've stuck through this entire book only to be met with this bullshit.

If you're looking at things you don't like about yourself or that you want to change about yourself, consider yourself lucky to be one step farther along in your journey to be able to see those faults. That means you're growing and learning!

Have you met the blissfully ignorant person who assumes they are perfect because they are too inexperienced to know differently? (Oh, hi teenagers). Being blessed with self-awareness, experiences, and knowledge means sometimes you're going to look at yourself and not like everything you see. Actually, this sums up life perfectly. Each stage in life we learn more and have to grow more.

That's not a bad thing! Well, it's a bad thing when you turn it into self-loathing and not self-improvement. Or it's a bad thing when it turns into crippling self-doubt. To prevent that, you need to first be grateful that you're aware enough to see your faults. And then you need to take a closer look and make sure you're not just being an asshole to yourself. If it's something you really do need to improve, then get after it. If you're just being a jerk to your precious self, then acknowledge it and apologize to yourself. And go back to the self-love chapter and start over.

I give you permission to marinate in the juices of whatever was in the glass we were staring at while acting philosophical. It's not half full or half empty. It's there to be consumed for your pleasure. Pick up the glass and drink it. And then pass it over to me because I'm on this journey with you and I want some, too.

FINISH THE DRINK.

19. REMEMBER WHO YOU ARE

Welcome to your villain era.

Do you remember who you were?

Before learning you had to rid yourself of body hair to be respected?

Before learning that quiet means acceptance?

Before learning that a voice of justice incites rage instead of spurring protection?

Before being taught that you had to offer value before you can have worth?

Before you had to ace tests in school to get access to opportunities?

Before you set career goals?

Before life felt like a daily cycle of repetition?

My ancestors used to laugh and shout, dipping their naked bodies into brisk, blue waterfalls. The water would rush over the cliff, providing them with a musical backdrop of a soothing, soft roar, relaxing their minds and their bodies.

My ancestors knew how to heal themselves and others from the land. They would lie on the forest floor and soak in the energy pulsing under the ground. They knew which plants to pick to cure illnesses and to help their village. They dedicated their days to foraging lazily through the forest, collecting what they needed along the way. They would laugh and sing while exploring their part of the earth, enjoying the sounds and sights of their oasis.

My ancestors took their time walking through forests, caressing plants and tree trunks, as they breathed in their surroundings. They would inhale the life force of the forest into their lungs and let it spread through their bodies.

My ancestors lounged on cliffs and watched the sun disappear for the day. They'd take in the reds, oranges, and pinks of the fading light. They would sit there until complete darkness fell on their shoulders like a blanket, letting the night embrace them. Listening to the creatures who had woken up for the night.

My ancestors would gather around fires and tell stories of the women in their families. They'd talk about what they learned from them. They'd appreciate the knowledge and love that was handed down and would voice their gratitude for younger generations to witness. And for the trees to hear. And to help the bees settle in for the night.

I know these stories are true because I once ran with these women. I once floated, laughing, in a pool of water with them. I once sat on a cliff, leaning back on my hands so I could look up at the sky, smiling, watching vibrant colors fade into night. I once walked through the forest, running my hands along dark green leaves, talking about who I loved, who needed healing, stories from the day before, and listening to the stories of my sisters.

This is who I am.

Deep down at my cellular level, this is who I am. I am free. I am knowledgeable. I am loved. I am understood. I am accepted. I am connected to the land. I am loved by the wind who tells me secrets. I am embraced by the fog who escorts ancestors back to our realm for another hug.

I know who I am deep down. When I'm outside attending to my herb garden, I remember who I am. I remember who I am while soaking in the bath, starting a fire in the fire pit, tangled in bed with my partner, mixing a tea blend for my friends, and while lighting candles and burning bay leaves. I know who I am and I will not forget myself again.

Life is a series of reality-altering moments. Yes, there are huge events that you planned for and catastrophes you would never imagine, but others are small, seemingly insignificant moments. Where you're standing at your window on a winter's morning, holding a cup of coffee that's still too hot to drink, and letting the heater warm your legs. Or you glance up in time to catch a look on someone's face that gives you a five-hundred-page story in less than one second. Or you read something that stops you in your tracks as you greedily digest the knowledge download.

Your life is full of amazing things, even in the most mundane moments. Think about what you've been through and what you've accomplished. But mostly, think about—and remember—who you *are*. You are a powerhouse of possibilities. You are the gentle breeze that follows a terrible storm. You are laughter that bubbles up out of control and impossible not to join in. You're that first bite of triple-chocolate, five-layer cake covered in a glossy ganache. You're a terrifying protector of those you love. You are the smirk that gives away a story before words can. You are a goddess full of beautiful, horrible, amazing, scary things.

While you start to remember who you are, the world will continue denying your truth, attempting to hold you down. And unfortunately, the hardest part of our villainous journey is that often it's those closest to us who want to hold us down. That's why it's so important to remember *who you are*. While abusers are grabbing their pitch forks and screaming "villain!" I want you to *remember who you are*. The nastier they get, the more scared they are. And a woman speaking her truth, telling her story, is scary as shit.

But you're not just a woman. You're a goddess. You're terrifying and your protection isn't weak. So, no matter what . . . *remember who you are.*

I give you permission to . . . wait, girl, are you still looking for permission? Honey, the permission is yours to give. You own all your next steps.

Welcome to your villain era, you sexy witch.

ABOUT THE AUTHOR

Ashley is deeply passionate about empowering women to recognize their worth and reach their full potential. As the founder of a Digital Marketing Agency and with 24 years of experience writing content, Ashley's goal is to help female business owners grow their confidence and embrace being "seen" online—an essential step for any successful business. With her sharp wit, natural sass, and expertise in empowering women to take control of their online presence, she's crafted a book she describes as more of a survival guide than a typical self-help read.

When she's not writing or running her business, she loves spending time with her amazing family—who she lovingly calls her personal superheroes—and her Doxiepoo, Tango (who looks like the cutest little rag mop). She's also fond of the critters in her backyard, from tiny crawlies to fluffy hoppies. In fact, you can usually find her by a fire, no matter if it's 100 degrees or freezing—it's her slightly ridiculous, but perfectly Ashley, obsession. (And yes, she knows "hoppies" isn't a word, but she insists it should be).

www.villaineragoddess.com

ACKNOWLEDGMENTS

Good grief this book was scary to write. I wouldn't let anyone read it except my sister, Jessica, and my editor, Katrina, until I felt it was "ready" for more eyes. My sister knew I'd be airing all kinds of drama and supported me the entire time—that takes a strong woman. If you've made it this far and you're actually reading the Acknowledgements, then please send love into the universe for my dear sister.

I don't know what I would have done if I hadn't met my editor, Katrina Schroeder, and received the unlimited amount of support and guidance she offered the entire time. The thing with editors is that you forget they're not your best friend, soulmate, and sister from another mister, because you get that close. So, Katrina, thank you for answering all of the Snapchats and text messages like we once shared the same womb. Because in my mind, we did.

The Fiction Lab is for fiction writers and this amazing group took the time to critique my non-fiction chapter submissions. We'll always have our JC Penny family portrait photos from WriterCon. Love you guys. Hey authors, visit thefictionlab.com.

And lastly, Sony, thanks for cooking supper. My husband never once asked *if* I was going to finish my book, he asked *when* I was going to finish my book. "Awoooo" (That's wolf pack speak that only he will understand).

www.ingramcontent.com/pod-product-compliance
Lightning Source LLC
Chambersburg PA
CBHW061749120626
46550CB00005B/1937